# 11

## steps to brand heaven

# 11
# steps to
# brand
# heaven

*The ultimate guide
to buying an
advertising campaign*

# Len Weinreich

**KOGAN
PAGE**

Kogan Page Limited
120 Pentonville Road
London
N1 9JN
UK

Kogan Page Limited
163 Central Avenue, Suite 4
Dover
NH 03820
USA

© Leonard Weinreich, 1999

British Library Cataloguing in Publication Data

A CIP record for this book is available from the British Library.

ISBN 0 7494 2894 5

Typeset by Patrick Armstrong, Book Production Services
Printed and bound by The Bath Press, Bath

*To Muggsy, 1984–1998*
*Our much-missed Bearded Collie, who snoozed in the study*
*as I cursed the keyboard.*

# CONTENTS

# FOREWORD

## FOREWORD TO **UK** EDITION

Len Weinreich is a copywriter. He comes from a time when creative people wrote English, not just put ideas on paper. I met him when he joined Hugh Burkett, leading to a successful management buyout from Saatchi & Saatchi. I knew of his work and particularly admired his Sir Robert Mark campaign for Goodyear.

I was in trouble (this happens to marketing directors) on Baileys Irish Cream. He made a film for me, *Cat* we called it, and the brand has not looked back since, nor has my career. Len is a great salesman, his presentations never less than compelling. Often times, the ads are great too. When I read this book, he stands before me again and I learn again. You don't have to be Jewish, but it helps.

Anthony Scouller
Marketing Director, United Distillers and Vintners UK
1998

## FOREWORD TO **US** EDITION

This book is bad news for most advertising agencies. Weinreich unmasks how agencies pitch for business and gives clients some useful cues on how to cut through the nonsense and select the right agency. He provides a practical point of view on how to get the best work out of the winner. Most dangerous of all, he provides a sophisticated set of parameters for distinguishing good advertising from bad. All in an easy manner that will make clients laugh all the way to the meeting. Since it takes a good client to make a good agency, I believe this book can make a real contribution to advertising effectiveness.

Les Delano
Executive Director, The Lowe Group
New York, 1998

# ACKNOWLEDGEMENTS

To: Tony Scouller, progenitor-in-chief; Barry Bryant, for yelling encouragement from the touchline; Pauline Goodwin, subtle wielder of velvet glove; Derek Atkins, the kestrel eye of copy-editing; Lester Delano, urbane counsellor; Harriet Potter and 6-week-old Isabel for coaxing and cooing; Jenny Blythe, industrious delver; to the editors of stable-mates *Marketing*, in whose pages some of these words appeared in altered form, and *Campaign*, for limitless quoting rights.

Never to be overlooked, my family: Dr Jonathan Weinreich, for cyberspatial navigation; Deborah Weinreich, cheerleader and scourge of inefficiency; and their mother, my wife, the formidable Frances Weinreich, whose patience, guidance and intuition remain, as ever, indispensable to all of us.

While scouring the planet to locate permission for reproduction rights, it would seem that some rightful owners are lost in historical fog and others held shackled inside legal vaults by cheerless legal guardians.

Fortunately, the world is full of extremely co-operative people, so, thanks to: the Stanley King Collection, NYC for Nixon's The One; David Cowperthwaite for permission and co-writer Martin Hodges for the Pentax proofs; librarian Barbara Walker at the Kennel Club for mega-champ Saredon Forever Young; The Mentholatum Company US (owners of the registered trademark) for the Fletcher's Castoria ad; Graphic-Sha Publishing Company Ltd, Tokyo, for the 50s Hudson and Starfire car ads; Barnaby's Picture Library in London for the Botswana cave paintings; Marina Luri at Donna Karan New York; R J Reynolds Tobacco UK for the Camel poster; Graham Truscott at Rolls-Royce for the Ogilvy classic ad; vp Patricia Yoder at Avis; Lisa Hirst at D&AD and writer John Kelly for the Call for Entries proof; the Central Office of Information and art director Steve Grime for the headlamp road safety ad; vp Gale Griffen at Bestfoods US for permission to reproduce Levy's Rye Bread and Nucoa margarine ads; and DDB–Needham NYC for supplying the Levy's transparency.

Deep breath. More thanks to Benetton for the over-affectionate horses; Jeanette D Sindle at Colgate–Palmolive for the ancient 'Honey I got the Job' ad; the Alfred Dunhill Museum and Archive, 48 Jermyn Street, London SW1, for the smashing E S Turner painting; DDB–Needham NYC for my favourite VW press ad; Vlasic Foods International for Swanson's TV Dinners; the Ford billboard comes from *The American Billboard, 100 years* and is reprinted with permission. The great Margaret Bourke-White photograph is © *Life* magazine and the Pepsi ad, New York City is reproduced with permission of photographer Robert Landau; I'm also grateful to Dover Books for Gustav Doré's irate Moses; the photo of the Booker Steed container truck is by the author, as are the two rough scribbles. Abject apologies to anyone I have omitted or overlooked. Sorry, sorry, sorry.

*I am very easy to please.*
*Just give me the best.*

Edward Kennedy 'Duke' Ellington

# INTRODUCTION

The peerless Tony Brignull, one of the very few copywriters to achieve superstar status, told me a story about his addressing a seminar of marketing directors at Bedford College, University of London.

Emboldened by after-dinner cognac, Tony enquired whether they all felt they were fully qualified to judge creative work.

'Yes,' they said, flooding the single syllable with conviction and certainty.

'Are you sure?' he asked. 'Because every week I see dozens of scripts and layouts and I have to go home and think about them really hard to sift the promising from the dross.'

'Yes,' they said, 'we're absolutely sure.'

'In which case,' continued Tony, 'had you been in Paris at the beginning of the Impressionist period, would you have bought masterpieces for a pittance, or would you have rubbished them along with the main body of critics?'

The room fell silent.

This book is unusual. It is the first primer for marketing directors to be written without an ulterior business motive. Previous books about buying advertising have been written as agency promo packs tipping the wink – 'Come to my place and we'll see you right' – and usually promoting a new variant of communication theory posing as agency philosophy.[1]

I don't have an agency to promote. No axe to grind. Nor do I have any nostrums to flog. What you see is what you get: a distillation of forty years in the adbiz, from oily rag in client's advertising department to the stratospheric overview of a Euro-executive creative director.

Some successes. Some failures. All instructive. But, of all the lasting lessons I've learned, three override everything else:

1. *Whatever promises are made, there are no certainties.*

2. *Nobody knows anything (borrowed from Hollywood scriptwriter William Goldman).*

3. *No cat will ever do anything you want on camera.*

Step carefully. And good luck.

[1] It was Chris Wilkins who once suggested that agencies with agency philosophy should have agency philosophers, men with long grey beards, sitting in a room and thinking deeply.

# STEP I: REVELATION

One night in Chicago, during the late 1930s, the incomparable Art Tatum, almost blind genius of jazz piano, entered the crowded Panther Room at the Drake Hotel to attend a set by Thomas 'Fats' Waller.[1] Waller (no slouch at the keyboard and one of the most influential pianists and composers in jazz) stopped playing and whispered into the microphone, addressing the audience confidentially: 'Ladies and gentlemen, I play piano, but tonight God is in the house.'

1   Also known as the 'charmful little armful', he called his breakfast whisky 'my liquid ham and eggs'.

'*God is in the house.*' Peer recognition and respect on a monumental scale. But does it ring a familiar bell? Are you unaware that your arrival in the foyer of an ad agency provokes a similar effect?

Cut to foyer. The receptionist's greeting has a musical lilt and, as she takes your coat, her captivating smile is extra bright. The deceptively understated *ikebana* arrangement on her desk is extra fresh. In all likelihood, the reception carpet had, seconds before, been subjected to an extra snog with the vacuum cleaner.

The newspapers and magazines are fresh and unsullied. But you don't get a chance to soil or sully them because an agency board director, wearing sincerest smile and crisp Armani threads, is poised to escort you to the conference room. More senior managers, together with an electric *frisson* of expectancy, greet you as you enter. Throughout your stay in the building, you will be breathing the air of privilege, the closest attention being paid to your every utterance.

Does it come as a shock to learn that, in the world of advertising, you are 'God'? Sorry to break the news like that, but you have to consider the consequences, because it follows that the agency is your church, carrying your message to your congregation. It reassures the faithful and converts the sceptics. The agency account team? Priests to follow your bidding. The place is alive with cardinals, bishops, abbots, missionaries and seers. You have the ability to control creation itself, commanding scribes and artists to sing your praises. Every one of them thinks of you as a god.

But deep inside, you are aware of the real truth: you are not a god; *the brand is God.* You are GCROE, God's Chosen Representative On Earth, invested with full licence to play proxy God.

However, it would be unwise if you allowed this revelation to go to your head and carry you away. Therefore, before you start claiming total omnipotence or start throwing thunderbolts, you should realize that you are not the sole proxy deity but one among many. Your actual standing – or P/O/V (Paradise/Olympus/Valhalla) rating – can be measured. It depends on:

◆ *first and foremost, the strength of your brand;*
◆ *your budget;*
◆ *your individual power; and*
◆ *your personality.*

Improving your P/O/V rating means showing visible improvements on all four aspects. Yet:

- ◆ *brand strength depends on the ads, the market, the climate and all sorts of events outside your control;*
- ◆ *budget depends on the financial director of your corporation (unless you're the boss as well);*
- ◆ *your individual power depends on your status in your organization; but*
- ◆ *your personality depends on you, your decisions and your actions.*

It is possible to improve your P/O/V status by concentrating on improving your performance in that fourth sector. Once you're skilled, the others will follow and fall into line, and before you know it you'll be well on the way to omnipresence and omnipotence.

But first, as in all spiritual matters, you are required to take a journey

You must be initiated into the Mysteries. You must learn from the Masters. You must study Holy Writ.

This much is clear: people who pay money to run advertisements in the media (unless they are governments attempting to prohibit something), crave to channel the desire, admiration, will and faith of a sizeable chunk of the public.[2]

*The public.* How many dubious actions are committed, claiming support by public opinion? And what is public opinion? In some areas of endeavour people are downright fickle, while in others they are highly predictable. The only reliable fact is that

2  Of course governments also crave love and admiration but, as with stern parents issuing orders, threats and penalties (and breaking promises), affection evaporates quickly.

they act according to all the dictates of human nature, unchanged since *Homo pithecanthropus* got off all fours and started shambling *erectus*.

The 'highly predictable' bit is easy. Most people crave certainty and worship beauty and power. When beauty and power occur together, the result is *awe*. If the combination occurs in human form, the charismatic creature is immediately elevated to iconic status. As ordinary punters, we are prepared to make almost any sacrifice to possess elements of charisma. Ask any passing snake-oil salesman: a promise of beauty, power or certainty at a decent price is assured of our attention (and possibly our money). Provided our attention is attracted in the first place. Provided provenance is authenticated. And provided miracles are demonstrated.

The odd thing about being a marketing person, spring-loaded to sell, is that you are constantly being urged to buy, buy, buy — ideas, notions, projects, schemes, space and time. Making choices raises stress levels, meaning, for people who prefer a sedate life, that the softest option is rejection (even though it may be supremely irrelevant that the act of rejection is totally divorced from your preferences).

Acceptance, on the other hand, triggers the automatic unrolling of a minefield where straightforward advance is ill-advised; any obviously beckoning route is bound to be laced with booby traps; signposts (if any), will be misleading; and a bad move can mutilate a budding career.

It would help if you burrowed into the recesses of your memory and cast your mind backwards to a time when you were an underling, junior of juniors, shadowing the then GCROE,[3] fresh in this game and new to the scene (I hope this is not too traumatic). Indulge in a little nostalgia and we'll conjure the scene together.

There you are in the ad agency's stylish boardroom, conference table covered in notepads, coffee cups and storyboards, atmosphere vibrating with high drama. The creative director has resumed his seat after presenting the agency's creative recommendations. Layouts and ideas have been exposed, all exhorting *'buy me, buy me, buy me'*. Throats clear noisily and someone on your side of the table thanks the agency politely for their 'obvious effort and hard work'.

Oh *shit*. Judging by expressions (post-presentation relief tempered by expectation of criticism) across the table, the ad agency team is hungering for favourable review.

As the details of the presentation flood back into your mind, you negotiate the torrent by mentally executing a manoeuvre midway between doggie paddle and drowning. As your memory back-flips through a frantic recap, your instincts are straining so hard that they hurt. Let's see: the agency's analysis of your problem was perceptive but radical. *Damn*. Their recommended action is ingenious but unorthodox. *Blast*. And although the creative argument is daring, it possesses elements of risk. *Hell*.

3    God's Chosen Representative On Earth, just in case you'd forgotten.

7

It was not supposed to end like this. As the presentation progressed, a sort of picture began to emerge and you could almost visualize the sort of advertising they were going to produce.

And that was when they unveiled their solution. It was not what you expected, or even imagined. As your heart elides a beat, your epiglottis gulps and you crave invisibility, you discover forgotten religious beliefs and beseech the powers-that-be that your opinion should remain unconsulted. *Fat chance.*

This is the point at which you become aware that every face in the room has turned expectantly towards you. *Holy shit. You have been invited to comment first.*

Predictably, your first instinct is to imitate a goldfish with breathing problems, but, as the first icicles begin to crystallize in your circulatory system, you become acutely aware that the pile of cardboard in front of you could possibly be 24-carat gold. Or Grade A garbage. You draw a deep breath and, depending on how your personality and reactions have been hard-wired, your view emerges as:

◆ *The cautious diplomat,* playing for time by mumbling something coherent, perhaps even significant, but definitely non-committal. The phrase 'see what we learn in research'[4] might even be muttered.

◆ *The prosecuting counsel,* where, with forensic flourish, you expose innate flaws and argue that the inherent risk in the approach has the ability to undermine chances of success, so

**4** I am not about to rehearse all the hoary arguments against research ('a crutch, a substitute for taking a real decision' etc, etc), except to suggest that it's most shaky when testing the unfamiliar. In my experience: when asked 'Would you want a remote control for your TV?' respondents who had never experienced a remote control replied: 'Absolutely not: I can walk across to my set and change channels by myself.' When, a few years later, a different question ('Would you ever give up your TV remote control?') was posed, respondents were horrified at the suggestion. And the responses were exactly the same before and after the introduction of automatic dishwashers. Consumers (except for certain discrete cadres, to be examined later) are a conservative bunch who offer qualified support to any change that doesn't affect them personally or financially. Incidentally, judging by the evidence about us in the form of other people's ads, research is hardly great shakes at picking winners — or even at spotting flaws.

sentencing the entire enterprise to an unceremonious funeral in black polythene sacks.

◆ *The radical visionary*, identifying the core truth in the idea, which you support with fervour and insulate from any future assaults by Cautious Diplomats, Prosecuting Counsels or Mute Goldfish.

Hope shouldn't be jettisoned quite yet. We could suggest a plausible explanation to justify even a trainee god's conduct at first presentation.

For the sake of argument, let us assume that the agency has hit the button with a superb presentation. Displaying inspired teamwork, they responded to your company's brief with coruscating brilliance. Their analysis was devastatingly accurate. Their inspired answers possess the ability to solve all your problems, propelling your brand to stardom while trouncing the opposition and tipping it into the nearest rubbish bin. Even in this utopian state, the toughness of your predicament must not be underestimated. While you are still reeling from exposure to an emotionally blockbusting advertising campaign, your management is anticipating a lucid critical response.

A gasp of startled amazement is not enough. *'Cor blimey!'*, while deeply felt, does not carry sufficient gravitas for the occasion. Look at it this way: you are being asked to articulate rationally (and off the cuff) as though the campaign were expressing purely functional issues,[5] even allowing for **Proposition No. 1: Never trust anyone who can articulate logically after professing to have been profoundly moved**. If you are unfeasibly lucky,

5   *Private Eye*, the fortnightly satirical magazine, created an enduring institution in 'Pseuds' Corner', where published critical opinions are submitted by readers to be exposed to justifiable ridicule. The most common submissions are absurdly high-flown rhetoric about abstract issues, suggesting that suspicion of instant opinion is healthy and instant rational response to an emotional issue must be shallow. This reflects **Proposition No. 1**.

inspiration will strike and, in ringing phrases, you become an eloquent advocate for the cause. If you are not very lucky, you could find yourself waffling or joining the vote to ditch the campaign.

Even so, although gut feeling and articulation are not usually a matched set, gut feeling is as reasonable a criterion as any other for judging ads. At the 1998 British TV Awards, jury president James Lowther of the M&C Saatchi agency recommended that jurors judge commercials by the reaction of the hairs on the backs of their necks. *Rigid bristles?* Give it a hearty commendation. *Listless follicles?* Bin it. In the end, it is the only way. Unfortunately, commerce lacks vocabulary for epiphanic experiences.

Blame everything on my youthful conditioning as a chorister, but I have always been struck by the similarity between advertising presentations and religious services. The parallels are remarkable: the gathering of the devoted congregation, the reverence in the presence of the brand, the ritual incantations, repetitions, sermonizing, ceremonial and responses.

Religious services evolved to provide a format for human beings to commune ('interface' in corporate-speak) with a deity, a way of channelling spiritual and emotional issues. And it prompted me to wonder whether the advertising presentation provides a similar service when business meets art. My conclusion is that it all depends on faith.

Is this a bizarre view? Not really, if you accept that every real decision in advertising ('Will it run or won't it?', 'Should we appoint them as our agency?', 'Should we support this brand with a bigger budget?') is fundamentally emotional, because every real advertising decision is ultimately about faith. Can you guarantee a return to your financial director? Can you predict an outcome accurately? You can guess and you can call on experience. You can judge by form; you can feel it in your water. But we all know that, in the end, it all depends on faith. Faith in the brand. Faith in the market. Faith in the agency. Faith in the ads. Faith in the campaign.

In the light of that view, let me float **Proposition No. 2: Buying a campaign requires faith rather than rationality**.

Every marketing novice learns that various tycoons throughout the past century[6] have been credited with the observation: 'Half my advertising budget is wasted – but I don't know which half.' Carefully inspected, that observation says a mouthful. It's a braggart's way of saying (1) that he's got a lot of money to spend on advertising, (2) his ads stimulate sufficient interest for him not to bother too much about science, and (3) he has unbridled faith in his judgement and the strength of his brand.

**6** Gordon Selfridge, Lord Leverhulme, F W Woolworth… Take your pick.

Faith has been defined as '*the acceptance of the intellectually unacceptable*'. If my argument strikes you as sacrilegious, go no further. But consider this: without faith in brand or product, would there be any investment in promotion or advertising (already identified by successful, hard-headed millionaires as a wasteful process)?

## HANDY ANALOGIES

Up till now, the competitive nature of the business has compelled marketing folk to poach their analogies and metaphors from sport and military affairs, inevitably leading to a lot of macho posturing. Recent evidence suggests that faith and religion might serve us better.

Recent surveys indicate that British families are now more likely to venture out to shop on a Sunday rather than sit down to the traditional dinner of roast beef and two veg. Or attend church.[7] And in *Much Depends on Dinner*,[8] Margaret Visser's prizewinning book about the anthropology of an ordinary meal, the author mischievously suggests that supermarkets are the modern equivalent of cathedrals.

Furthermore, only a few pages ago, you were informed that you, yourself, may well be referred to as 'God'. The metaphor is infectious: don't marketing managers talk about a brand's *Bible*? Aren't advisors called *Gurus*? Are we not all seeking *The Holy Grail*? Isn't the brief regarded as *Gospel*? What are research interviews, but the *taking of confessions*? What is favourable brand-switching but *conversion*?

Allow me to introduce **Proposition No. 3: Faith in a brand requires equal faith in its myth.** Is it true that Rolls-Royce once sent a mechanic to mend a breakdown in a remote corner of Eastern Europe, and admonished the customer six months later when he requested the bill, saying: 'Sir, Rolls-Royces do not break down.'? Is it true? Frankly, it does not matter. The fascination

**7** Car washing hangs on a little longer.

**8** Penguin Books, 1986.

with the story lies in the *possibility* of its being true (if it could be, then it might be. If it might, then it is). You don't have to like something to believe in it.

Now, consider various long-running advertising campaigns that have burrowed into your brain, without your approval and, in all likelihood, against your better judgement. For instance, Singapore Airlines, featuring an almond-eyed temptress as every male business traveller's exotic odalisque, promising ecstasy on the wing. Or Impulse, where a lady's spray deodorant transforms ordinary nerds into sexual harassers, frenziedly brandishing bouquets. And then there is Cadbury's Milk Tray, with testosterone-fuelled stuntmen executing perilous black-clad gymnastics to satisfy ladies' dependence on confectionery. Whether or not you like them, you will find that you (definitely not one of life's suckers) have accepted the fantasy, pretty well undiluted. Indeed, liking or disliking ads has scant bearing on how deeply the repeated myths penetrate your consciousness.

Thus we have **Proposition No. 4: Myths defy logic**.

## CONTRADICTIONS AND PARADOXES

Are brands contradictory? Certainly. Brands also often present paradoxes. Suspending disbelief (difficult enough in most circumstances) in order to promote a myth requires credibility. If you intend to lay claim to miraculous powers, it helps if your credentials are well established.

### SUSPENDING DISBELIEF

Mercedes-Benz can claim anything about engineering and be believed; ex-Eastern bloc cars such as Lada cannot – yet. In the UK a few years back BMW ran a spoof April Fool's Day ad in which it announced a new gizmo that inflated tyres automatically should the pressure fall. I am sure that readers studied the announcement with fascination because it could have been true (and they were probably disappointed that it was not). BMW's heritage of innovative design allowed them to kid the public on that subject and be forgiven, not a route that many manufacturers could emulate.

### PRODUCING MIRACLES

Let's assume that your intention is to astonish your audience, shake them from their sofa torpor and knock their socks off. One route is to opt for a fantasy treatment (the British Airways 'Manhattan' commercial[9] rushes to mind) and unleash the money supply (central break, *News at Ten*, every night for a week). Unfortunately, the effect of unremitting hype can actually begin to weaken credibility (imagine the reaction if Moses had reprised the splitting of the Red Sea for seven nights in a row).

The first time you witness the spectacle of the island of Manhattan touching down at London Heathrow, you are speechless with awe at the scope of the idea. The second time, you begin to sense the irrelevance of BA's message to ordinary mortals. The third time, the flaws become apparent as you spot the joins. The fourth time, you sniff the arrogance of the argument and start recalling tales of alleged dirty tricks and derring-do. Conjurors

9    Corporate Campaign Formula No. 1: grab massive statistic and dramatize it. In this case, the annual total of passengers flown by BA was roughly equivalent to the population of the island of Manhattan. So, instead of a 747 with lowered undercarriage, we had Manhattan being guided into Heathrow, an image not unlike the landing of the mother ship in Spielberg's *Close Encounters of the Third Kind*, but with none of the tension. And none of the intended sense of awe.

seldom repeat tricks identically in rapid succession because familiarity is a fast-breeding reactor of contempt.

In contrast, Apple Macintosh's '1984' ad (a far superior predecessor to 'Manhattan', offering news and promising hope rather than empty thorax-thumping hype), was screened once and once only. All subsequent public screenings were at the climax of international award ceremonies where '1984' seized the top prizes to ungrudging roars of peer group approval. One could only shake one's head in admiration at (1) the agency's sophisticated understanding of media event as drama, (2) the heft of the client's *cojones* and (3) his faith in the campaign.

Conventional marketing training states that having lots of marks on the media schedule is very good; very few is bad. Terrific if you can afford it, but what the trainers neglect to tell you at marketing college is this: when a single spot, oft-repeated, causes *ad nauseam*,[10] you are spending money to negative effect.

10  Latin for being sick of ads.

Nevertheless, whatever you do, remember this: after a period of time, whether you like it or not, successive brand campaigns compound themselves into a myth.

## DO NOT RELINQUISH MYTH CONTROL

Myth? Yes, myth. Myths regarding:

◆ *the brand's history ('The best car in the world...', 'I dived to the spot twenty years later and there was my Rolex Oyster Perpetual, still maintaining perfect accuracy through the movement of the current...');*

◆ *the brand's origins (France: food and perfume, yes, but electronics, no; Italy: fashion, pasta and cars, yes, but cosmetics and tobacco, not really; Germany: cars, definitely, but clothes and booze, not really. And are you actually ready to buy Estonian fashion items?); and*

◆ *the brand's effect on consumers ('I actually feel better/more attractive/more powerful when I immerse myself in…', 'I deserve a treat/reward and will indulge myself with…').*

As captain of your brand's destiny, never permit control of its myth to be wrested from you. Brand myths need constant servicing, with regular refreshment and make-overs. They require fine-tuning to accommodate current consumer behaviour and embrace current events (or, as novelist Geoff Dyer writes in a different context: 'siphoning the *Zeitgeist* into the action').

Look at it this way: your brand's future depends on whether or not consumers believe a number of things about it. And you know that all the things you want them to believe are totally rational. You would also prefer it if they held those beliefs about your myth with a certain degree of *passion*. Which brings us to **Proposition No. 5: Belief plus passion equals faith**.

Faith[11] is what you seek – faith of such an intensity that the faithful coalesce into a cult, a small group of committed believers. The history of every major religious and political movement indicates that if it's a mass movement you're after, you must begin with a motivated cult.[12] If you're really lucky, the cult should have your brand at the centre, because that's the time-honoured technique for starting religions.

11   Why has nobody ever named a company Faith Bulldozers ('We move mountains.')? Oh, forget it.

12   If the implications for launch advertising aren't making themselves clear, don't worry. Simply bear in mind that most people are slow to grasp significance and you can't please everyone at once.

## WHERE ARE YOU NOW?

At this point in the proceedings you're perfectly entitled to feel somewhat confused. On innocently picking up this book, you probably thought you were going to read something mildly instructive about choosing a campaign in an ad agency and suddenly you find yourself neck-deep in the business of promoting religions.

Myths? Faith? Cults? Religion? In dealings with clients, ad agencies tend to downplay the importance of emotion[13] and other deep feelings. Emotions, in this rational age under the benevolent dictate of accountants, don't figure on the balance sheet. Immeasurable at the best of times, they're near impossible to value.

You are also entitled to point out that the very idea of religion is boring. Not if you're God's chosen representative, it isn't. A goodly amount of people want to believe in *something*.[14] And, yes, religions are about moral values and all the rest, but are most attractive when they are accompanied by a sense of passion. When passion is absent, religions become intellectual exercises and distance themselves from common folk. When passion is spent, religions become boring, irrelevant and fade into the ether.

Incidentally, advertising has never been slow to apply the ciphers and representative symbols of religion and to whip them into use as clichés. A quick trawl through print and TV archives will reveal:

13  Hence the title of the first successful marketing textbook, *Scientific Advertising*, written by copywriter Claude Hopkins.

14  Or should that be *anything*? It could be that the tabloids are the new gospels because many folk give ecstatic credence to reported sightings of Elvis Presley (the *King*) in Las Vegas supermarkets. We are witnessing a cult in the making, complete with shrine (who could have chosen a better name than '*Graceland*'?) and holy relics. Allow me to be a prophet: after a handful of well-placed miracles round about 50 years hence, there will be a First Church of Elvis Presley (his name is an anagram of L-I-V-E-S and E-V-I-L-S. And L-E-V-I-S, yet another icon. Spooky isn't it?). And, of course, ditto for the late Diana, Princess of Wales.

- *devils (temptation);*
- *nuns (easily shockable);*
- *monks (stumbling into drunkenness);*
- *vicars (bumbling or clap-happy);*
- *angels and priests (hostages to temptation);*
- *haloes (symbols of purity); and*
- *the coy upward peek (an intimate relationship with the Almighty).*

Nearly all are used with a knowing, greetings' card kind of cuteness.

We've arrived at that point where you (and any agency folk who might be surreptitiously peering over your shoulder) could well be sniggering up your Prada sleeve. Scoff away, but ponder this point for a moment. Marketing and advertising folk, rational, empirical and modern to their carbon fibre cutting edges, are prone to dismiss any hint of mysticism, necromancy or even more conventional religion in their lives. *Superficially.* Because in my experience ad agency folk are nearly as superstitious as thespians and theatricals[15] (most superstitions originating with the prehistorical need to avert the evil eye).

15    Don't whistle backstage, don't mention the name of 'the Scottish play', etc.

'Don't need bad luck,' they snigger nervously, as they consult their daily horoscope. 'I can't wear my unlucky tie to this morning's pitch,' they fret to the wardrobe mirror. 'Mustn't tempt fate,' they mutter, as they sidestep the builder's ladder. Napoleon Bonaparte enquired, before promoting an officer to the rank of general, 'Is he lucky?' And the Kevin Spacey character, Roger

'Verbal' Kint, says in the film *Usual Suspects*: 'People don't believe in God. But they're scared of Him.' Even Carl Jung gets into the act with: 'To embrace myth and to readmit primitive religion in social behaviour is not to flee modernity, but to face up to it.'

So, **Proposition No. 6: Knock on wood**. Simply because you never know. They might all be right.

# PROPOSITION REPRISE

### Proposition No. 1

*Never trust anyone who can articulate logically after professing to have been profoundly moved.*

### Proposition No. 2

*Buying a campaign requires faith rather than rationality.*

### Proposition No. 3

*Faith in a brand requires equal faith in its myth.*

### Proposition No. 4

*Myths defy logic.*

### Proposition No. 5

*Belief plus passion equals faith.*

### Proposition No. 6

*Knock on wood.*

# STEP 2: THE CULT

As the brand's earthly representative, you'll be supremely aware that the key to true success is the formation of a brand cult. As marketing tasks go, cult formation is the most difficult of all. And while you can learn from case histories, you can't copy them.

## THE POWER OF THE BRAND

All brands, whether they are cat litter or cognac, require reverential handling. As GCROE, you should expect (and some clients even demand) agencies to echo your own approach to the brand.[1] Brands often portray themselves as possessing potent forces. Some ('*Double Diamond Works Wonders*', '*Heineken Refreshes The Parts Other Beers Cannot Reach*') have boasted supernatural powers. Many have claimed to work miracles in rejuvenation, healing or sexual attraction.

Even in their death throes, brands have an ability to retaliate. Need any British reader be reminded of the notorious Ratner effect, when Gerald Ratner, boss of a jewellery chain, attempting a conference joke, publicly belittled his merchandise (and its consumers) by calling it 'crap'? The insult made headlines, lost him his job and scuttled the Ratner brand.

Scuttled the brand? To damage a brand is unfortunate, risking jobs, careers and profits. To lose a brand is disastrous, junking years of goodwill and immeasurable investment in time, money and human effort. In balance-sheet terms, it is tantamount to

1 Some clients go to incredible lengths to indoctrinate their agencies: I once encountered the story of a pet food manufacturer who insisted that everyone on its agency account team should own pets. The account director, a lifelong victim of fur allergy, was forced to maintain a phantom cat and retailed cute pet anecdotes at meetings. He was unable to invite the client home.

Car manufacturers prefer their creatives to drive. For years my star writer on a massive automobile account was a non-driver. Every time he was invited to try a new model on the test track he would essay some pathetic excuse like 'twisted my ankle on the dance floor last night'. Did I mention that he was also unable to dance?

demolishing a productive factory full of high-quality plant and firing all the highly skilled staff. But to throw away a brand bearing *your own name* and by your own error of judgement is unforgivable. It's uncertain whether or not Gerald Ratner's exercise in televised hara-kiri was prompted by iconoclasm, but the effect was the same. And, judging by the subsequent media flagellation, humiliating one's own brand publicly is tantamount to blasphemy. So, **Proposition No. 7: Brands are strong medicine and carry powerful ju-ju.**

Let me illustrate this further with two tumblers of clear liquid I poured out earlier. I promise there is nothing up my sleeve. The first is filled with filtered grain alcohol diluted with distilled water – hardly exciting. Then, into the background appears a bottle with the label reading 'Smirnoff'. Hey presto, the liquid in the tumbler has a personality. It has emotional values. It is a brand that people believe in. People don't believe anything about *vodka* except that it makes you drunk quickly. Yet, against all intellectual acceptance, people believe a mass of things about *Smirnoff*, many of them irrational. Those who believe most fervently constitute a cult.

No brand has ever succeeded without first creating a cult of followers. Once a cult starts forming, the brand is marked for star status. And it doesn't even need to be in a glamorous category.

The second tumbler is also filled with clear liquid – this time plain water. Emotionally neutral. Now add half a chemistry set compressed into a tablet. The liquid begins to fizz. Allow it to settle, and then drink it, enjoying the pleasant refreshing effect. If you know that the tablet is stamped 'Alka Seltzer', it (and all the emotions connected with it) will cure your headache, indigestion, heartburn or hangover. Strong medicine indeed.

Regular purchasers of Alka Seltzer have made the brand *iconic*. Its advertising and associated promotions are its *iconography*.

With the sole objective of inducing awe, the top religious powers throughout the ages have cannily employed the best available artists, architects, musicians and writers to produce iconography and religious propaganda. In more than a few cases, they have produced sublime art with the ability to move emotions. Nothing has changed: if you want the best iconography (as evidenced by every billboard and TV screen), you need the best artists. Only they are able to dramatize your brand's core values in a manner that taps the right emotions. Only they have the ability to produce brand iconography in order to refresh and replenish the brand myth. And 'core brand values'? Could that be marketing-speak for 'soul'?

## BRAND HEAVEN

What you're currently reading here concerns the necessary steps for the ultimate pilgrimage. But before attempting the journey, why not allow yourself a privileged preview of life behind the Pearly Gates. Upmarket estate agents would describe Brand Heaven as 'a desirable neighbourhood', but it is reserved for those elite brands that have located their particular Holy Grail, that ecstatic state when the brand's intended image and consumers' perception are identical.

Brand Heaven is sparsely inhabited, but all the residents are pretty familiar. Peering through the wrought ironwork, we can see Levi-Strauss, Sony, Ferrari, VW, Rolex, Armani, Coca-Cola, Marlboro, Boeing, Mars bars, Porsche, Microsoft, Nike, Kleenex, Alka Seltzer and Heinz.

Admittance is gained through elevation by the cult followers, that loyal group persuaded to have faith in the brand's cause. Cult followers believe in a brand because somewhere at sometime it has touched their lives with some degree of understanding, passion and charisma. Passion is crucial. Without passion there is no conviction, and without possessing conviction, you will never be able to convince anyone else of a product's worth.

Passion persuades people to accept impossibilities. Charisma is important too, but more difficult to achieve. More than straightforward appearance, it is about personality, character and glamour. Some brands are naturally glamorous by birth, luck or age, while others have to work to achieve it, though it can seldom be designed: the workaday Land Rover, for instance, has more charisma than any other Rover model.

Once you own charisma and passion, you're permitted to ask the directions to Brand Heaven. In the meantime, here's the map (a world exclusive):

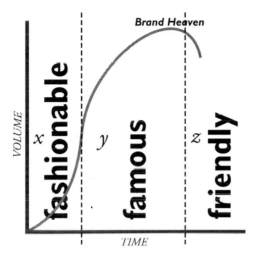

**Figure 2.1** *The S-curve*

## THE ROUTE TO PARADISE

Is this familiar? It should be, because you are looking at the S-curve. And Brand Heaven is located where the curve begins to bend downwards.

The S curve is a handy guide to brand life and development, graphically charting birth, growth, maturity, decay and death (the very stuff of cults and religion). Without much skill, you too can track your development and your proximity to Brand Heaven on the S-curve.

The S-curve can be extremely revealing. For instance, instead of viewing it as tracking sales volume over time, consider it as a series of stages in the brand's relationship with its consumers. In that way, you gain an interesting insight into a brand's communications requirements. And, if we grant each of the distinct $x, y$ and $z$ phases a description, we can re-evaluate brand experience in a new light.

Time calibration is elastic: in the case of, say, Guinness stout, it is close on two hundred years and continuing. In the case of General Foods' 'Space Dust' confectionery, it was six weeks from start to finish (never underestimate the evanescent appeal of novelty, particularly a fizzy powder that explodes on the tongue).

### THE X PHASE: BEING FASHIONABLE

Label the $x$ section, with its steep rise, *'fashionable'*, the $y$ section, with its shallower increase, *'famous'* and call the slowly declining $z$ section *'friendly'*.

In section $x$, the market is tiny and many brands succeed *in spite of* their promotional efforts because the product is innovative and excellent. And no matter how ill-executed, the sheer act of advertising, of making a public sales message, cannot help but raise awareness and stimulate demand. The creative quality of the stimulus is almost irrelevant (and frequently ignored) as consumers rush to possess something perceived to be highly modish and desirable.

Fashionable consumers may not be numerous, but they are influential. They are neophiliacs, lovers of the new (Sony calls them 'early adopters') and they wield immense influence as taste shapers. Claiming not to be influenced by advertising (although the sceptic in me bets they request Alka Seltzer by name), they influence advertising itself. But as they consume more of the brand, it passes into phase $y$, aka the 'famous' phase, and the phase $x$ consumers drop off and go after the next new thing.

Phase $x$ consumers are too cool to be doing what everyone does. They're exclusive and don't want to be seen wearing, driving, eating or drinking anything that the next lot is consuming. Particularly if they've been there, done that, etc, etc.

Here are a couple of secrets to attracting the $x$ group:

◆ *either be lucky enough to be selling the right product (for years, Porsche's advertising was unappetising while the product was mouth-wateringly desirable); or*

◆ *be seen to be effortless, restrained, hip and cool.*[2]

Not heavily into loyalty or long-term relationships, our $x$ lot raise fickleness to high art, but that doesn't mean that they (and their successors) are not vital to all our marketing efforts.

### THE Y PHASE: BEING FAMOUS

More fortunately, moving onwards and upwards, our $y$ consumers are loyal and make you rich, but they too are subject to human frailties. As they age, the brand might become too expensive for them, or irrelevant to their lives. They buy less and eventually disappear off the face of brand earth.

If you haven't continued to make the brand relevant to new $y$s, you will drift on to the deadly $z$ zone, where everyone knows about you, but they don't bother to buy you any more.

2    *Cool?* Like so many other terms ('hip', 'Big Apple', 'jive' and 'gig'), 'cool' is a word derived from black jazz slang. It means 'laid-back and knowing' (though not necessarily knowledgeable – that's 'hip') and an ability to keep even heavy emotional response contained under wraps.

'Cool Britannia'? Don't ask me. It all began with a Ben & Jerry's ice cream flavour.

### THE Z PHASE: BEING FRIENDLY

Brands slipping into *z* have been known to possess almost 100 per cent awareness, but it doesn't mean a thing if consumers have turned their backs. So we have **Proposition No. 8: Fame isn't everything**, and **Proposition No. 9: Friendly is not necessarily good for business**.

As a brand, the Rolls-Royce car has 100 per cent awareness, but in recessionary times that doesn't help much and the owners can't do much about cutting prices to drum up extra trade. Similarly, the old Woolworth's had 100 per cent awareness (remember 'the Wonder of Woolies'?) but scant respect, and this eroded profits.

The challenge of *z* directs a brand either to its nemesis or its renaissance. It demands careful consideration of future plans and subtle manipulations of strategy.

It's easy to tell when a badly managed brand has hit the *z* phase: its advertising gets overwarm, cuddly and sentimental, the antithesis of *x* cool.

However, sometimes fashion itself can help certain brands to find themselves achieving second leases of life on the S-curve.

There are quite a few brands that started out as one thing, then became something else *as well,* when a new generation of consumers (or marketing experts) discovered that they had suitable class or style emblems: Harley-Davidson and Brylcreem, to name just two. And when the *x* crowd set the fashion for old fountain pens and wristwatches, manufacturers had to re-jig production for retro-style products. When the *x* crowd decided the country-side was due for revival, four-wheel-drive vehicles became urban snob badges and the country Barbour jacket became common garb in English cities.

The rag trade is littered with similar tales. Remember the naval duffel coat that became the mark of every CND-supporting student? Or, more recently, the Australian stockdriver's Drizabone wet weather coat that became a fashion accessory? Or how French youth scramble for Fred Perry tennis shirts, hardly a major fashion item in the UK? Or the rise of Doc Martens, a working man's boot that became a female fashion statement? And learn from Levi's, essentially working men's gear that became the indispensable wardrobe item of the young.

Except that Levi's carried a built-in time bomb. Users became so loyal that the habit persisted as they aged. Now Levi's are worn mostly by people over forty *because of* their 'youthful' appeal, damaging the brand's youth credentials every time a wrinkly buys a pair.

## WHAT LESSONS DOES THE S-CURVE TEACH US?

The S-curve teaches us that, if the mythology isn't carefully nurtured, the portcullis of Brand Hell is only a couple of blocks from the portals of Brand Heaven.

It also teaches us that, if a brand has been seriously wounded and requires major surgery, you need to go back to *x*. Perceived core brand values need reassessing. The brand's relevance to its target market needs to be redefined and redramatized.

For instance, after the embarrassingly dreadful 'Guinless' campaign of the early 1980s (possibly the worst indignity heaped upon a famous brand. My toes still imitate startled armadillos at the memory), Guinness fired the agency responsible and appointed a new shop to repair the damage. Quite correctly, the new agency revived and refreshed Guinnesss's core brand values: presenting a natural product with a heroic history in a *sturm und drang* commercial that celebrated the virtues of flame, rain and the natural countryside. It was a virtual re-launch and literally a rebirth through fire, set to reassure Guinness drinkers that their favourite tipple had not lost its marbles. It went a long way to restoring the crass vandalization wreaked upon the brand.

Not only does the S-curve give you a fix on your location, it also gives you a steer on your direction. Any future progress depends on your intellect, intuition and experience. But before we pitch into the future, let us be armed by lessons from the past. So it's time to read and revise.

# PROPOSITION RECALL

## Proposition No. 7

*Brands are strong medicine and carry powerful ju-ju.*

## Proposition No. 8

*Fame isn't everything.*

## Proposition No. 9

*Friendly is not necessarily good for business.*

# STEP 3: GENESIS

**B**eing a brand's chosen representative on earth is not easy. Instead of relaxing by your private ocean, sipping an ambrosia *frappé* and never worrying about sunburn, you're a full-time supervisor correcting the eccentric wrinkles of creation and a part-time wrestler grappling with paradoxes.

Some paradoxes maintain an iron lock perilously close to heaven's front door. For instance, how did it come about that august religions (always holier-than-thou) turned themselves into brazen institutions? Positively shameless, they trumpet their origins with unshakeable confidence while promoting themselves as beacons of modesty, honesty and righteousness. Yet a few minutes spent in a well-stocked library reveals rickety frameworks of dubious evidence, mounted on shifty foundations of superstitious fog, held together with a sticky sense of communal guilt. It's a contradiction that teaches us three lessons:

1.  Audiences crave explanations and guarantees of certainties – particularly from burning-eyed preachers with buckets of charisma.

2.  With the right amount of spin, moral and spiritual certainty are a formidable team.

3.  And yet, despite all the above, religions survive, even in these times of rampant materialism and contrary scientific evidence.

Seeking an explanation for the third point, how about this? When the job of hard-wiring our species was completed, we discovered that both of two custom options, Hope and Lingering Doubt, had been fitted as standard from the very instant we started measuring time.

## MEET THE CAVEMAN

But, as you know too well, if you'd been walking about in the palaeolithic era, a ready-packed luncheon snack for sabre-toothed tigers, you too would have sought a reason for existence in a world under ever-present threat of inclement weather, darkness,[1] hunger, disease[2] and merciless predators with powerful jaws. The origin of almost everything we do and believe can be understood tracing our development back to our ancestors in caves or makeshift shelters.[3]

Existence,[4] based on hunting, was tough. Hunger was a daily event because handy shrink-wrapped antelope joints weren't readily available for the pot. Life was also spent on the run because our nomadic hunting ancestors had to migrate with the herds. Occasionally, owing to either climate or catastrophe (or a combination of both), the herds decamped or vanished and the hunters and their families starved.

Secure in the knowledge that human nature has never changed, we can be sure that our ancestors, led by the oldest and wisest clan member, probably besought the forces of nature to restore the food. In short, they performed some of the first religious ceremonies and uttered some of the first prayers.

1. In later times, when ships plied the Mediterranean loaded with amphorae of olive oil, it was more for illumination and rather less for lowering cholesterol.

2. Do you realize that it wasn't until the third decade of the twentieth century that doctors were actually able to cure anything?

3. In other words, at fortune's first downturn, you would have been down on your knees worshipping thunder (big noise in sky = displeasure of big force), begging forgiveness for any affront you had caused. Did you know that a single trip in an ambulance can turn an atheist into a zealot?

4. Nasty, Brutish & Short – a good ad agency name: '…no, sorry, I can't put you through to Mr Brutish, because he's busy garrotting his double-glazing client.'

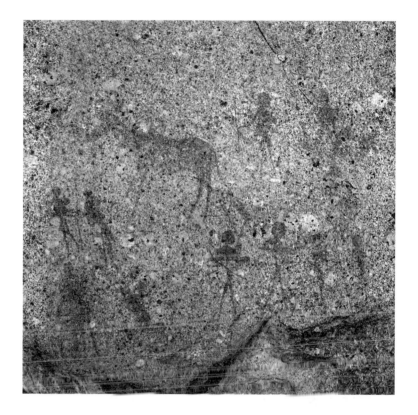

Weeks might have passed. Younger members of the clan began to forget how to recognize an antelope. However, a sensitive chap, attempting to quell the gnawing hunger in his intestines, noticed ridges in the rock wall of his cave resembling the outline of an antelope. Guided by the lines, he sketched a brilliant representation on the cave wall, rendering hoof and horn affectionately with natural pigments. Next day,[5] as luck would have it, our sensitive artist came face-to-snout with a wandering antelope. With speed that would shame the plunging hawk, news of the miraculous

5    Would you believe?

**6**  A miracle is only a natural event with a brilliant sense of timing.

**7**  It's a better theory than an emergent trend in interior decoration.

encounter[6] spread through the clan, stimulating a frenzy of applying antelope[7] representations to cave walls on the theory that, if it had worked for him, it might work for me. Overnight, the antelope returned to graze the plain, initiating high season for antelope-steak barbecues.

Later that evening, lolling around embers and contentedly gnawing bones, the oldest and wisest member of the clan declared: 'This was not a coincidence, it was a miracle. The power of prayer is good.'

The original sensitive artist pondered the declaration for a while and, experiencing a *frisson* of paranoia, wondered whether he was not being written out of the script. Sketching in the sand with a burnt stick, he commented: 'You're absolutely right, of course. But I'm convinced that my artwork was a vital component of the rite, which I have now called *Sympathetic Magic.*'

'He's got a point,' murmured the others, impressed by technical phraseology.

'Maybe our sensitive artist has a precious gift,' suggested another tribal sage, stifling a burp.

Heads nodded all around the fire. 'Yeah,' they agreed, dislodging vermin from their abundant fur. 'We never looked at it that way before.'

Hey presto! By magic, we have witnessed the birth of the Antelope Cult, completely equipped with a brand new high priest and lawmaker.

As the sense of power dawns on the High Priest, he dons his sacred antlers and barely draws breath before declaring his first acclamations:

*Fellow Antelopers, I have decreed that the antelope symbol be our clan system's holy emblem. It is our fetish, our icon. Icons are holy. Holiness is a mystery. Only I am sufficiently sensitive to understand and penetrate the depths of the mystery. Indeed, from this moment onwards, only I am permitted to supervise the drawing of icons on cave walls.*

*Any icon raised without my approval and blessing is heretical and bad medicine.*

*And furthermore, as all my time will be spent communing with the natural spirits, supervising iconic mysteries and managing cult affairs, hunting will be a taboo occupation, an unclean pursuit and totally unfitting for me. In other words, I shall not hunt again, but you will bring me food. In fact, I expect to be compensated for my work with a regular guaranteed percentage of antelope, prime cuts only.*

*I have spoken.*

'Ah, men,'[8] responded one of the clan's matrons, luxuriating in the agreeable sensation of being replete.

8  Be grateful that I spared you 'deer, deer'.

37

Judging by the graphic evidence of cave walls across the world, covered with paintings, we might assume that, whether by coincidence, happenstance or shrewd manipulation, the clan had discovered a winning formula and that the cult was a hit.[9]

**9** And that, as a guess about how organized religion began, is probably as good as any.

However, I would step into further uncharted territory with this suggestion: picture one member of the clan paying closer attention than the others. Rapt in contemplation regarding powerful images and religion, his astuteness is prompted by the realization that *'This can be exploited for profit.'* Alas, although we may never know his name, his legacy survives in the form of the Palaeolithic Doctrine of Propaganda, which has ruled supreme (and almost unchanged) for the following 99,950 years.

It is instructive to examine the Palaeolithic Dogma:

◆ *A large illustration of a warthog on a cave wall equates to a juicy warthog picked off on the veldt.*

◆ *This large illustration becomes an icon.*

◆ *An icon raised to mighty proportions will excite awe in the multitude.*

◆ *And the multitude will be thus encouraged to rush off and hunt the holy warthog at the nearest megastore.*

◆ *Should the multitude prove stiff-necked and unresponsive, then the assault should be doubled (and redoubled) on the multitude's apathy by doubling (and redoubling) the size of the icon.*

◆ *And doing that again and again until all available space is filled.*

The icon may be a picture of the product, the brand name or, frequently, a combination of both in juxtaposition. A palaeolithic dogmatist would have believed that such an icon possessed mystical power, explaining why the icon was very large indeed (and repeated as often as possible).

If the response to these stimuli was muted, the caveman yelled even louder for attention, throwing larger quantities of money at the problem, urging the priest/painters now in his employ to increase the pressure and increase the size of the icons. Note that there would have been no attempt at persuasion (just wave it in their faces) nor any attempt at seduction (simply drag 'em in by the ponytail).

Palaeolithic communication was brusque and direct because it was based on the simple (but fallacious) nostrum that *stimulus equals response*.[10] Consequently, any failure of communication was blamed on the consumer, the media, the quality of reproduction or the capricious weather. But never on our cave-dweller himself.

To the caveman, advertising was a purely functional act and therefore wrote its own rules. Caveman Rules still operated for innumerable years when the advertising industry was young.[11] And they were so strikingly effective that the basic rules petrified into immutable dogma (some of which is still quoted mindlessly to this very day).

Unashamedly displayed in public, the caveman's techniques (and successes) were impossible to ignore and endlessly copied. One of the greatest inventions was the strip cartoon (*slow pan:* Greek vases in the British Museum; *mix to:* the Bayeux Tapestry; *mix to:* Giotto's frescoes in Padua), a means of shifting narrative from the aural to the visual,[12] the abstract to the concrete, the temporary to the permanent.

Strip cartoons told stories that illiterate people could comprehend, yet were able to retain their attraction even when literacy grew. Advertising latched on to comic strips very quickly and some images (*rapid montage:* Charles Atlas's 9-stone weakling; 'Speedy' Alka-Seltzer; Tootsie Rolls and Horlicks ending the deprivation of 'night starvation'[13]).

But, like all the caveman's other brainwaves, comic strips proliferated for every brand. As did billboards, book-matches and

10 The only people who still give the equation any credit are incurable control freaks. Can you recall the last time you did anything you were told to do?

11 The business probably began earlier than one would imagine. When you think about it, advertising is the second-oldest profession, because the elder sibling must somehow have had to publicize services and tariffs.

12 Indeed, how do we know that cave paintings weren't an early form of strip narrative?

13 Those *were* the days – when advertising could actually *invent* medical conditions.

*The cavemun was no longer alone*

all other splendid new ideas for spreading the name. His dominance had been challenged and, suddenly, he was no longer alone.

Caveman tactics, devastatingly effective when geared to *solus* media superiority, were in danger of backfiring. Where he had pioneered a system of creating a demand that only he could satisfy, competitors seized advantage of the burgeoning demand and limited supply and nibbled at the edges of his market. Now the media was congested with similar brands, conflicting claims, improved designs at lower prices, miracle ingredients and better product performance. His total allegiance to the Golden Rule[14] was beginning to cost him dear as he found himself spending an increasing percentage of his margin to be heard above the clamour.

14    He who has the
        gold, rules.

The unacceptable conclusion, *'spend more to be heard less'*, was beginning to have a deleterious effect on his deepest instinct, the most sacred belief of all and always unspoken: *'Nothing must come between me and profit.'*

To develop our theme, we have to leave him for a moment as he squats on his haunches pondering the setback to his fortunes.

## THE UNHOLY DOCTRINE

For *afficionados* of cruel irony, here's cruel irony: Charles Darwin spent most of his adult life in ill-health and acute discomfort. And he's the man who instructed us that evolution favours the fittest. As though determined to provide his own example, he successfully demonstrated that 'fittest' is not interchangeable with 'strongest', but rather 'best equipped to survive'. Evolution favours brain cells as well as rock-hard biceps and a six-pack abdomen. Strategy, cunning and intelligence can defeat brute force. On any scale.

And that short homily should prepare you for a slow, deliberate pan to a different group of people in long shot. As we zoom in closer, details inform us that these are very different folk indeed. These are the people who had decided that hunting, a wasteful and inefficient method of obtaining food, should not be the sole method of filling the larder. Furthermore, the nomadic existence of moving homes every season to track the herds was exhausting, dangerous and life-sapping.

We are witnessing the result of the application of brain cells. Through the careful observation of seasons, they had noticed that nourishing berries, roots and grasses could be grown almost precisely where they wanted them to grow, a decided improvement on foraging. They also discovered that, by careful tending, they could raise crops to feed their families and livestock, ensuring fresh food in season and any surpluses preserved for winter. The first glimmers of the concept of *convenience* were appearing.

By living closer together, security would be improved. Employing their intellect rather than their instincts, they had invented cultivation and settled society. And these reformers settled in and lived happily ever after on the fruits of their sophisticated analysis.

OK, OK. The analogy needs no further labouring. Let's get back to business. Through experience, our cave-dweller had developed a set of inflexible rules, the Holy Doctrine of Imposed Aspiration. It comprised ten taboos:[15]

1.  *Exclude nobody*. The appeal must be all-inclusive and addressed to everyone.

[15] I shall resist the temptation to call them anything else.

16  When Paul Leeves was a very young art director, he once commented: 'In the sixties all the ads showed boys and girls in white clothes and feather boas zipping up and down the King's Road in white Mini-Mokes.' He wasn't far wrong.

17  A style adored by French clients – see any French commercial..

18  Particularly if it's a hair-care commercial. And most particularly if it's a *French* hair-care commercial.

19  Check any 1970s 'Martini People' and Coca-Cola commercials.

2.  *The imperfect is forbidden.* Everyone portrayed in the vicinity of the brand or product must be flawless and bacteria-free.

3.  *Ignore society.* Any human being inhabits a parallel universe where society's rules and standards are ten years behind.

4.  *Ignore individualism.* As (3) above, but applying to style.

5.  *Never show unsanitized youth.* If the brand is aimed at young people, then young people must be shown in profusion and having polite fun.[16]

6.  *Never be negative.* Brand images should be associated with energy, so that young people should be jumping up and down to a lively piece of music.[17]

7.  *Laughter is forbidden.* Character portrayals will be cleared of any hint of irony, cynicism, iconoclasm, subversion or wit.[18]

8.  *Never look downwards.* Interiors, wardrobe, children and holidays must be pitched higher than the intended market's experience so as to stimulate aspiration.[19]

*Notice the subtle underlining of Mom's*

9.   *Reality is dirty.* Real life is an intrusion.

10.  *Never overestimate the taste of your audience.*

All this makes excellent sense if you think that being patronizing is the way to makes friends, customers and consumers. The Holy Doctrine of Imposed Aspiration is a one-way instruction about how you should think, feel and behave in the vicinity of a brand. Switch on your TV, tune into a commercial station and feel the Imposed Aspiration flooding through the screen. It has the effect of saddling the wretched consumer with the advertiser's view of life. Rather than addressing the brand's relationship with the consumer's real needs, it reduces the brand's function to one of being a fashion accessory. Not part of your life, but part of the way that you live.

Not that it's even you. It's someone the advertiser and agency think you might like to be.

Please do not underestimate the severely negative effect of Imposed Aspiration. Consumers who find the message unacceptable can be seriously alienated. And those who find it naff might, in an act of backlash, assemble into an anti-cult.

My sermon begs an example: so here comes Exhibit 1, sounding a hollow fanfare to mindless enthusiasm. While all the components are present (the brand is sympathetically portrayed and all the traditional patriotic triggers, from eagle to flag, are in evidence), it shows a medium and a message falling flat. The poster attempts to impose what its supporters would like you to think.

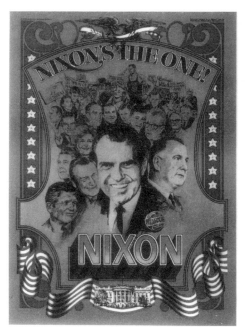

Exhibit I

At no point does it persuade (although I have to admit a fond-
ness for the pensive vice-presidential crook, sorry, candidate, over
the presidential candidate's left shoulder). At no point does it go
any deeper than a cosmetic skin job. And the effort to rouse
excitement is so frenzied that you can almost sniff the reek of stale
sweat.

The Caveman Club believes 'I'm available, buy me' is sufficient persuasion in itself. It has instinctual fetishes and taboos
about emotional issues: women love babies, men like big breasts,
and everyone loves puppies. Everyone harbours identical patriotic feelings.

The Caveman knows all about enlisting attention with emotional triggers by making unadorned appeals to greed, lust, envy, slapstick, sentimentality and gluttony. Through experience, he knows that repetition locks a message into the brain. Through his accounting system, he is learning that repetition has become very expensive. Through shrewd instinct he knows that half his money is wasted. And that's it. That's all he knows.

## SEE THE LIGHT

Expert in communication, the Church of Cultivation knows a whole lot of other things, expressed in the utterly rational statement of its belief in Rewarded Comprehension. The creed comprises just eight points:

1.  A stiletto can be more effective than a bludgeon.

2.  Wit can lower defences (and even disarm).

3.  Flattery and conversation are skills to sharpen.

4.  An understanding of the lure of myth and the potency of romance is needed.

5.  An appreciation of the stimulating powers of art, drama, music and literature is also required.

6.  Plants requiring pollination in order to survive stimulate insects with a colourful flower and reward them with nectar.

7.  A stimulus unnoticed is a stimulus wasted.

8.  For a stimulus to engage its audience, its primary function is to draw attention to itself.

Armed with this formidable knowledge, the Cultivated Communion is better equipped to overcome consumer resistance. It can manipulate a broader selection of emotional buttons and cultural levers to elicit more complex responses to all manner of stimuli employing art, wit, music and literature.

### REWARDED COMPREHENSION: A DIVISIVE HERESY

Had it not been for my friend Mike Zagor's repeated insistence, I would have overlooked P G Wodehouse's *Summer Lightning*, and might have missed the author's advice, eminently adoptable as our **Proposition No. 10: The first lesson an author has to learn is that he cannot please everybody**.

This is a point well-spotted by the Cultivated Church, who had already learned the impossibility of converting every living being to its cause. Therefore they narrowed their scope and entered into a more profound conversation with their target market, making them feel privileged to be more deeply involved.

Fewer, but more committed, people prefigure the formation of a cult. Less waste means lower cost and greater effectiveness. Demolishing convention attracts notoriety and a greater share of fame and status than traditionally applied larger budgets.

The Caveman's appeal is directed at the instincts. The Cultivated Church's appeal raises the level of sophistication and engages the mind. Instinctive reaction versus intelligent decision. Makes you think, doesn't it?

Once the in-joke/allusion/reference is absorbed and understood, the consumer is granted a bout of self-congratulation as a reward. And the communication cycle is complete.

'Tosh,' you say.

'*No,*' I respond in contradiction and, as though demonstrating my thesis by feat of legerdemain, I produce yet another poster from the hat, using precisely the identical stimulus and subject as the previous example.

*Exhibit 2 'Let me make myself perfectly clear'*

Exhibit 2 takes a different tack but approaches the reader with subtlety and stealth. Wielding a scalpel, it probes into the murky suspicions of ever-hovering guilt, confirming shiftiness and mistrust. Where Exhibit 1 invites ridicule unintentionally, Exhibit 2 applies it intentionally.

Exhibit 2 also contains what advertising creative people call 'an idea'. Which brings us to a proposition flood. **Proposition No. 11: Advertising with ideas is better remembered than advertising without ideas. And Proposition No. 12: The communication where you work out the meaning is the communication you remember. And Proposition No. 13: The communication you remember is the one that gets acted upon. And Proposition No. 14: If you're constructing the perfect mousetrap, it is vital that you leave room for the mouse.**

*Leave room for the mouse?* This heretical notion, revealed by the Cultivated Church, was reviled by Caveman orthodoxy, a tradition that refused to countenance fresh beliefs.

Some of us are old enough to remember the BBC radio interview with the President of the Flat Earth Society the day after the first images appeared of our planet photographed from outer space. It was plain to hear that the President, surveying the shreds of his belief, was in shock. Dispirited he might have been, but not defeated. He managed to croak, 'It's still early days, nothing's conclusive yet,' into the microphone.

Whole constructs have been built on erroneous beliefs. Failing systems are supported by dubious facts.[20] Rigidity in corporate

20   In the 14th century, Giovanni de Dondi designed a clock of astonishing complexity to demonstrate the movements of the moon, the sun and the planets. Using a series of cogs within cogs, he endeavoured to explain all the planets' eccentric orbits. Why we have forgotten de Dondi, while Copernicus is celebrated, is that de Dondi, with one large cog, made the sun rotate about the earth.

approach causes stultification and brings down an entire edifice. Or, putting it yet more bluntly, even corporate rules can be wrong. Do I hear the sound of alarms and sirens? *Corporate rules can be wrong?* Sorry about that, but someone had to say it. And parables hasten on their way.

*Illustrative parable number one.* There was the marketing director of a very large food company, who commented on seeing the rough-cut of the commercial: 'Why isn't steam curling above the drinks container? We have a rule stating categorically that all beverages give off steam at all times.'

'There is no steam,' I explained patiently, 'because the beverage in question is orange flavoured and best served chilled.'

Shifting uncomfortably in his chair, his sole audible response was a low growl, like a malign but retreating Rottweiler.

*Illustrative parable number two.* I was once introduced to a man reputed to be London's top restaurant guru. He was having problems (basically, no covers) with one of his establishments and I met him on site at his large, glitzy restaurant in Mayfair. 'Just had it refurbished at huge expense,' he said, with a broad gesture towards an expanse of Louis XV boudoir about the size of a small prairie: acres of gilded chairs, pale peach walls, sparkling crystal and starched napkins. 'It'll fill itself,' he promised.

With an imminent general election, we proposed a polling night party and ran a few ads that stimulated bookings. Post election, it was back to the empty, echoing prairie. Inevitably, the restaurant was sold and a new management team moved in. Out went the prissy furniture. In came odd chairs and tables. The peachy walls were distressed and covered with an eclectic collection of art. Louis XV was forgotten as the entire room took on the aspect of an unruly, though not unwelcoming, study. The restaurant was renamed 'Langan's Brasserie' and was never empty again.

The moral of these two parables? **Don't ever be deluded into believing in your own infallibility. You might have been right every single time up until now, but sooner or later you're going to be wrong** (worthy of becoming **Proposition No. 15**).

Having enjoyed successes because he was first in the field or had a genuine product advantage, the Caveman engraves his experience onto tablets of stone and calls the results 'Rules'. Or 'corporate strategy', or 'mission statement'. Many organizations are heavily locked into rigid disciplines, some of which are patently barmy,[21, 22] because people with mortgages haven't summoned the courage to modify, question or defy them. Often, the larger the corporation, the more silly the communications rules. Dogma, I'd call it.

## DOGMA AVERSION

Dogma brooks no interference, dissuades initiative and stifles talent. Did you know that the Soviet Union forbade its scientists to make use of Quantum Theory because its reliance on the probabilities (not the certainties) of subatomic events contradicted Marxist–Leninist dogma?[23]

**21** I once worked on a luxury fountain pen brand that had been bought by a US armaments conglomerate. They insisted that, for synergy's sake, the US armament conglomerate's logo (nothing to do with the pen's brand name) was featured in fountain pen commercials. We eventually won the argument.

**22** The agency was forbidden to use the word 'family' to address the target market of a brand of national chain stores because the marketing director felt that the actual owning family might feel that it referred

**23** See the article by Hugh Aldersey-Williams in the *Sunday Independent*, 10 May 1998.

Born of a sense of infallibility, dogma inevitably leads to arrogance. Arrogance inclines you to lose touch with trends and behaviour, lose relevance and become boring.

And don't take my word for it: harken ye unto the experts. Religions invite trouble when they get boring, as evidenced by a Church of England secret memo, written by one of the Synod's most senior policy-makers:

> … [the Synod] has become terminally tedious and is in danger of consigning the institution to irrelevance. The agenda of the Synod needs to be radically reshaped. We are a hostage to fortune on so many issues; our agenda is terminally tedious; we have become a refuge for the pedant, the bureaucrat and the bore… much of our agenda panders to the concerns of small minorities.

And the memo concludes:

> It is imperative that we recognize the way in which the whole synodical process can lock us into total irrelevance.[24]

24  The Guardian, 20 March 1998.

Dogma also damps down passion (to be popular and effective, a religion must stir strong emotions) and the end of that particular road is blandness. In the end, the arrogance of dogma breeds *hubris*.[25] And once *hubris* infects an organization, the instrument becomes the institution and corporate arteries begin to show signs of hardening. The results are very public because that's when corporations have ideas as brilliant as 'New Coke'.

25  Health Warning: the gods don't like *hubris*.

Seemingly, when it was at its most invulnerable, the dogma nut was actually cracked. The events are there for us to witness, but first you have to travel backwards to the late 1950s, the deeply conservative, ultra-prim Eisenhower era.[26] The place is New York City and the location, appropriately for anti-establishment activity, is underground.

It was a time of excessive paranoia (remember the McCarthy hearings?). It was a time when scriptwriters on the Chesterfield Cigarette Radio Show weren't permitted to announce that the Bedouins were arriving mounted upon camels, because Camels were a major competitive brand.[27]

26 A contemporary Hollywood film, *The Moon is Blue*, caused a furore by mentioning the word *virgin* in the dialogue.

27 I imagine, on the Camel Cigarette Show, no one was allowed to rest their bottom on a Chesterfield.

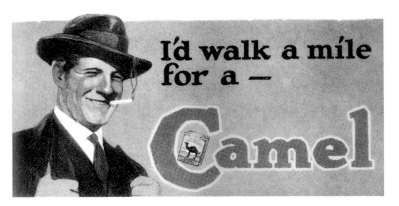

*At least, nobody could have written the same line for Chesterfield*

It was a time of excessive puritanism. The censorious Hays Office kept Hollywood lust under control. If a couple was in a bedroom, one leg in four had to be off the bed and on the floor. And no kiss was permitted to last longer than three seconds. It was also a time of authoritarianism in commerce and industry. The founding fathers of many giant corporations were still alive, still active and domineeringly despotic.

Under the combined forces of paranoia, puritanism and authoritarianism, advertising was in deadly earnest[28] and any spirit of freedom had to fight hard to draw breath. Hollywood's moguls and Madison Avenue Cavemen were in cahoots, promoting an all-American dream of peace and plenty. You know the sort of thing I mean, although this world before rock 'n' roll always bears re-describing: Mom, Pop, Junior and Sis, with a feisty puppy, all surrounded by small white picket fences in Burb Heaven, with Doris Day on the radio and no damned Commies or queers in sight. And, of course, you had to be white.

28 Contemporary novelists did not exaggerate: read *The Hucksters* and *Man In A Gray Flannel Suit*.

*Heaven on earth, courtesy of Madison Avenue* (©Graphic–Sha Publishing Company Ltd, Tokyo)

Based on their experience, the Cavemen of Madison Avenue prepared clear dogma regarding the craft of poster design, and a series of four immutable rules, caveman taboos for highly efficient billboards, had been carved in granite:

1. *The product is the totem: make it immense.*

2. *The logo is the fetish: make it really big.*

3. *Never use more than four words*

4. *Don't upset anyone.*

Then one day, without even scant warning, the rules changed. Overnight, the new gospel appeared in a single poster: the Levy's Rye Bread poster hit Manhattan's subway system walls, undoubtedly the most heretical piece of advertising ever issued, and split the world of advertising theory in two.

Indeed, it is worth spending a valuable minute or two examining this piece of communication simply to appreciate its flagrant four-fold insouciance in the face of accepted dogma:

1. Show the pack. *What pack?*

2. Get the logo up big. *What logo? What emblem? What trademark?*

3. No more than four words. *There are twelve.* Count them.

4. Don't offend anyone. *And they've referred to two minority groups and probably scandalized the entire WASP travelling public.*

*The most subversive poster in the history of advertising?*

Subsequent subjects included Chinese, Irish cops and Cherokee braves, all treated with so much warmth that no one could object.

The Levy's campaign was a watershed. Its use of imagery was tangibly contemporary. Drawing on American reality rather than the American dream, it didn't pretend to be idealized life. The humour was clear to all Manhattanites because it drew its energy from the urbanity and diverse multi-ethnicity of New York City.

The Levy's campaign was assembled by the most creatively influential advertising agency of all, Doyle Dane Bernbach, head-ed by the legendary Bill Bernbach. And (raising again the theme of dogma and rules) it was Bernbach who pointed out: '*Rules are what the artist breaks, the memorable never emerged from a formula.*' And, 35 years later, a Madison Avenue man said of Bernbach: 'I don't know how Bernbach felt about Picasso, but he's the Picasso of advertising. *He destroyed convention.*'

In Zoroastrianism, the fire-worshipping religion of ancient Persia, a major perk for the priesthood was a rip-roaring hallucinogenic sacred potion (recipe, alas, lost) called *soma*. *Soma* induced ecstatic visions and allowed the priesthood to divine the future. In the pre-Bernbach world, the most fashionable consecrated tipple in the marketing business was Caveman's Conventional, for which the recipe still exists:

*Cocktail Recipe of the Month:*

**Caveman's Conventional:**

Into a bottomless pit,
pour equal measures of
wishful thinking, received wisdom,
commonplace response,
blinkered prejudice and knee-jerk reaction.
Sprinkle heavily with caution
and
season with cowardice.

Although bland, you never become accustomed to the flavour and it leaves a nasty taste in the mouth. Ultimately, it does a lot of harm. Thus **Proposition No. 16: Stay as far as possible from Caveman's Conventional**.

It requires genius to smash dogma. But in order to revolutionize communications and enlighten the masses, it needs inside knowledge and someone who understands the business thoroughly – and who can then dismantle every component and completely rewrite the brief.

But now we're getting technical, so the time has come to be a little more thorough, break the flow and discuss a few definitions, with no stone unturned (for whatever may be lying beneath it). First, however, revise, revise, revise.

# REVISE, REVISE, REVISE

## Proposition No. 10

*The first lesson an author has to learn is that he cannot please everybody.*

## Proposition No. 11

*Advertising with ideas is better remembered than advertising without ideas.*

## Proposition No. 12

*The communication where you work out the meaning is the communication you remember.*

## Proposition No. 13

*The communication you remember is the one that gets acted upon.*

## Proposition No. 14

*If you're constructing the perfect mousetrap, it is vital that you leave room for the mouse.*

## Proposition No. 15

*Don't ever be deluded into believing in your own infallibility. You might have been right every single time up until now, but sooner or later you're going to be wrong.*

## Proposition No. 16

*Stay as far as possible from Caveman's Conventional.*

# STEP 4: ARTICLES OF FAITH

## ADVERTISING, FOR LATE BEGINNERS

*Q:* What is 'advertising'? (I said we were going to be thorough. And we have to start somewhere. Don't say you weren't warned.)

*A:* Confidently delivered advocacy on behalf of a brand, a service or an issue in communications media.

*Comment:* Advertising is the visible, paid-for part of a process that involves brands delivering coded signals that those brands are right for you.

But remember: 'advertising' is not one thing. Advertising can be a massive TV campaign for British Airways and a Saturday *Daily Mail* small ad for recreational rubber lingerie. It's a Dixons' list groaning with merchandise and a Government warning about road safety. It's an exhaustive demonstration of cooking utensils on daytime TV and a phone booth calling-card for a worker in the sex industry.

For the purposes of this tract, we'll restrict ourselves to addressing the subject of advertising as a brand-building instrument.

*Q:* What is an 'ad'?[1]

*A:* Mostly it's a substitute for personal persuasion.

[1] 'Ad' or 'advert'? Ever noticed that, whatever you choose to call it, your ad agency will use the alternative term?

**Comment:** Advertising's primary function is to raise awareness, alerting you to something you previously hadn't considered.

You're well aware how you can stumble across an unfamiliar word or unusual name you've never previously encountered and, once it's explained, it crops up endlessly. That's *raised awareness* and explains why tennis courts are fully booked during Wimbledon fortnight. Raised awareness prompts people to remember where they have stashed their tennis racquets.

**Q:** What, then, is an advertising campaign?

**A:** A series of ads that nag.

**Comment:** In Dr Johnson's opinion, '... *most people need to be reminded, not informed*'.

If you're out to raise awareness, repetition can defeat the apathy factor. It requires massive momentum to get punters off their butts to spend money on your brand. As luck would have it, the relationship between consumers and advertising is complex. Oft-repeated ads need to be a lot better than average, because consumers determine very swiftly whether or not they *like* an advertisement.

Early in the relationship, the audience forms an attitude regarding the communication. If the attitude is positive, they welcome its reappearance. If, however, the attitude is negative, they resent its presence on their screens. And the brain can trigger an involuntary switch-off to its message. So frequent exposure to an ad you dislike can serve to chafe rather than charm.

If that were not sufficiently dispiriting, yet another problem lurks like a lethal virus waiting to attack you: 'habituation'. If you put your finger on the table, you feel the table. If you leave it there, it eventually ignores the table. In other words, the laws of habituation deem that your message can become invisible through over-familiarity. To turn the cleverest ad into wallpaper, run it endlessly.

Habituation can only be fought with refreshed communications and new ideas. And the bottom line serves pretty well as **Proposition No. 17: Nobody counts the amount of ads you run; they just remember the impression you make.**

*Q:* What is creativity?

*A:* A means of making the nagging acceptable.

*Comment:* Creativity overcomes habituation and keeps communications fresh and up to date.

The advertising world uses people with creative talent to give nagging a palatable gloss, a sort of metaphysical candy-coating, by equipping it with a semblance of wit, charm, urgency or glamour. But before you convert or persuade, you have to attract. And the creatives' primary function is to shatter the target market's apathy.

Apathy is a negative force with a surprisingly massive drag effect. Consider this: how often have you promised yourself:

◆ *'I'm going to keep fit';*
◆ *'I'm going to learn a musical instrument';*
◆ *'I'm going to start dieting';* or
◆ *'I'll quit smoking';*

and then binned the whole enterprise before you've begun? Ask yourself why failed New Year's resolutions are such a universal joke? And why the metaphorical road to hell is paved with good intentions?

Now, allow me to suggest that, at this moment, it would be instructive to turn your imagination to a portrait of your audience. No, not the horde of humanity rushing towards you, eyes ablaze with gratitude, palms outstretched to accept your product. That's not them; that's wishful thinking. Your lot is slumped on a sofa eating tortilla chips, breaking off to slurp liquid out of a chilled can, while adjusting the duvet of apathy about its shoulders.

Using every means of persuasion at your command (as long as it is legal, decent and honest), you need to persuade them to change their habits to benefit your career. And all within a time-frame tightly constrained by budget.

Subject matter alone doesn't make an ad a creative *tour de force*. Sugar-coating is not enough. In the immortal words of star trombonist Trummy Young,[2] 'T'aint whatcha do, it's the way thatcha do it.' You need style, tone, energy and *chutzpah*.[3]

2    That's right, the Lunceford band. Then, later, with Louis Armstrong. Not a jazz fan? Too bad, there are so few of us left.

3    Being a Yiddish word, *chutzpah* comes ready-fitted with definition-by-anecdote. Young man murders both parents and begs for the court's clemency on the grounds that he is an orphan.

*Q:* So, what then is 'good' advertising?

*A:* (with a choice of definitions, depending upon which side of the fence you are standing): the *advertiser's definition* is that of a cost-effective, stimulating and positive communication of a brand's virtues; the *ad agency's definition* is that of an unusual (and therefore memorable) twist to a problem, well-executed and supported by sufficient funds.

*Q:* Why do we agonize over 'good' advertising?

*A:* Because 85 per cent of all ads are never noticed.

*Comment:* 85 per cent! Did you get that? Those moustachioed Edwardian tycoons referred to earlier were bragging about wasting 50 per cent. Our smug magnates would have soiled their spats had they guessed the reality was closer to 85 per cent.

How do we explain the 85 per cent level? Simply through **Proposition No. 18: Uninspired mediocrity is invisible.**[4] The messages are dull and the ads are boring.

[4] Even though the mediocrity might mention your name a lot and make the pack look terrific.

A night's TV viewing reveals some culprits (if you can be bothered to pay attention). Judging from the evidence on our screens (and billboards, and press, and radio), it would seem that companies still exist that believe in the power of their own will to overcome all opposition. Similarly, there are still cynical admen who will encourage, aid and abet their view before taking the money and running.

On the other hand (to be fair for a moment), a huge preponderance of ads is irrelevant at any time to most people. In the main, if an ad is irrelevant to personal needs, it is ignored. Unless you're in the market for a new fridge, you never notice ads for fridges. And it is a well-researched phenomenon that the moment you become most engrossed in car ads is when you have just taken delivery of a new car.

Also, the message of the ad might be totally relevant to the audience, but if the ad's attention-raising devices are poorly presented or irrelevant (as they often are), the message fails to get through and the ad is lost on its audience.

Further bad news regarding lack of faith emerges from the 1996 *Campaign* survey, conducted among advertising agency account planners, those oracles among the priesthood who stand astride the present and prophesy the future. For the past couple of decades account planners, wearing the sacred mantle of the omnipotent, have been opining about how, where, and upon what, money should be spent.

What were *Campaign*'s research findings? At this point, those of my readers of a nervous disposition should firmly grab some support, because only 17 per cent of planners agreed with the statement: 'Most advertising works.' Gosh, feet of clay. Perhaps they *are* human after all.

And that's only half the story, because life deals the advertiser a rotten hand. Every day, the average punter's conscious brain is bombarded by millions of visual and aural stimuli, mostly irrelevant to the punter's needs and ignored. But a goodly amount is competing frenziedly for a conscious (or even a subconscious) registration. In normal circumstances, your lonely message doesn't stand a hope in hell.

## READ ME

*Q:* Why this frenzied obsession with being noticed?

*A:* Because competition for consumers' attention is cutthroat.

*Comment:* And because £1 million spent on airtime around Christmas in the UK buys you *less than six minutes* to talk to your consumers, nationally. Six minutes to convince. Six minutes to seduce.

Not only has your story to be surprising, attractive, interesting and new, it must also be motivating, instructive, informative and full of promise. It had better be good – even for Mr and Mrs Apathetic, sofa-prone and bored, in front of the telly.

*Q:* So, how do we go about getting ads noticed?

*A:* (sorry about this, but the answer stretches over seven points; take a break and pour yourself a drink before you get more deeply involved):

1. *Ads get noticed by taking precise aim.* An art as well as a science, media doesn't always work to a cost-per-thousand rule of thumb. The famed Apple Mac commercial '1984' was a collection of superlatives: it was (a) produced at astronomi-

cal cost, (b) to be screened once and once only, (c) on the US's most expensive slot during the Super Bowl football final, American TV's biggest annual spectacle. Is it so surprising that the one-and-only appearance has never been forgotten?

2. *Ads get noticed by harnessing energy.* Almost any situation contains creative energy; it only needs to be tapped by the right talent. *The Economist's* poster advertising campaign has proved that it is possible to find energy, humour and drama in simple typographic billboards. John Smith's bitter beer proved it was possible to get pathos and drive out of two doleful men and a dog standing almost still in a Yorkshire pub.

Lazy creatives lean towards overt energy. How many times have you heard people extolling MTV and pop videos? Yes, I agree: pop videos and music are full of energy. No, I disagree: translating them onto the screen and appliquéing them onto a product does not necessarily communicate any energy whatsoever.

Energy is a by-product of conflict. It is released by revolution, anarchy and the shattering of conventions (you don't look to the Trooping of the Colour for energy). Apple's '1984' commercial, referred to earlier, was constructed to build mounting tension, which exploded into a massive climax, releasing huge amounts of creative energy (but you can only pull that trick once).

Energy is present in glamour, the unexpected, the unfamiliar, and unfamiliar juxtaposition. When Ray Charles (inspired casting as a glamorous icon, famously known to be blind) talks of preferring Diet Pepsi, while holding a can of Diet Coke in his hand (another icon), we are into a state of heavy iconoclasm and tangible energy.

When a furry Labrador puppy (all together now, *'aaaah'*) gets entangled with a roll of toilet paper, the energy comes from charm and concentrated cuteness, and the softness sales point is established. When further sales points are scored regarding the length and strength of the brand, you can only admire the ad (and when you consider that there's not much else acceptable for family TV in the way of a loo roll demonstration, then your admiration must be total).[5]

As the billboard campaign for the *Economist* has indicated, energy need be no more than the right selection of words. My favourite headline of all time was a small US ad of the sort dealing with human frailties. It stated simply and truthfully (and turned into **Proposition No. 19**): **'Haemorrhoids are a pain in the neck'**.

3.  *Ads get noticed by being interesting, surprising and relevant.* Fortunately for corporations who continually innovate, brilliant demonstration always makes dramatic viewing (exaggeration, where permitted by regulations, is useful too).

An American brand of freezer bags called Gladlox Zipper Bags ran a deceptively simple commercial. A presenter, filmed against a plain studio cyclorama, stood by a table explaining the advantages of a Gladlox Zipper Bag ('the

[5] Although the Japanese and Finnish toilet paper manufacturers do their best to stretch convention.

green seal shows that it's airtight') to an actress playing a sceptical housewife. She is resolutely sticking to her own choice of freezer bag. Meanwhile, in the background, scene-shifters are moving a telephone booth into the back of the frame.

*Presenter*: 'Would you allow us to lock you into that telephone booth with your current freezer bag full of angry bees? [*He holds bag full of angry bees aloft.*] Or would you prefer them in a Gladlox Zipper Bag? The green seal shows that it's closed really tight.'

*Housewife*: [Obstinacy fading under multiple sting threat as she nervously grabs Gladlox bag.] 'Change is good.'

*Presenter*: 'Bzzzzzzz. [Housewife almost has seizure.] Just kidding.'

Deftly applying surrealism, the Gladlox spot combines wit, genre parody and shrewd human observation for plenty of energy. And what's more, *the brand's conventional usage is never demonstrated: only its superior benefit.* Is that why the demo is so effective and so memorable?

4. *Ads get noticed by inventing indelible imagery.* Popular advertising mythology has it that 'make my logo bigger' is the traditional cry of the frustrated client[6] who is anxious to make an impression. If the logo is possessed of indelibility and crammed with significance (Coca-Cola, Sony, Kodak), then

6    Anonymous doggerel from pre-World War II advertising days (a handy list of the agents of anti-glamour):

If the client sobs and sighs,
Make the logo twice the size.
And should the client prove refractory,
Show a picture of the factory.
But only in the direst case
Should you show the client's face.

the client might have a point. However, only a few corporations are fortunate enough to own images that have developed existences of their own (the striding Johnnie Walker; *Playboy's* bunny; the Beatles crossing Abbey Road, Andy Warhol's lolling tongue for the Rolling Stones; the jolly Green Giant; the Homepride flour-graders; the VW Beetle; the MGM lion).

Difficult to create and establish, inventing indelible images is the most difficult trick in the art direction business. Yet, in the fragrance business, where punters buy images rather than scents, clients and their agencies try it all the time. Yves St Laurent was a dab hand at making brands stick (note Opium and Poison). But Coco Chanel, supreme mistress of the classic statement, rewrote the rule book with No, 5 and her re-invention of glamour.

5.  *Ads get noticed through perfecting timing.* Timing is indefinable. You've either got it, or ...

6.  *Ads get noticed through a consistent approach.* This is not as easy as it appears, yet consistency of approach is what separates great brands from also-rans. Ask Fairy Liquid, Heinz, Famous Grouse, Oxo, KitKat and, most of all, the immortal Volkswagen.

The most dangerous enemies of the consistent approach are young brand managers eager to make a mark on the world. Their philosophy would seem to be that a continuity fracture would benefit their careers. Over the years, we have witnessed the disruption of strong campaigns and the wanton destruction of valuable properties (remember the Bisto twins, the Homepride flour-graders, the Sugar Puffs Honey Monster, and Captain Birdseye), all sacrificed on the altar of temporary advancement. Later they are dusted off and called back into service to revive the fortunes of the brand when flagging sets in (in talented hands, almost any property could be totally reconditioned and made relevant again). And, by that time, the irresponsible culprit is presiding over a marketing shambles in a completely different company.

Thus we have **Proposition No. 20: To ensure consistency, young brand managers must be kept in line**.

7. *Curiously, ads attract most notice by appearing effortless.* Never allow it to seem as though you are trying too hard. And congratulations if you have already spotted the inherent paradox, that *the advertising industry tries to provide the public with intense experiences, delivered with the maximum of cool.*

Too much enthusiasm expressed for a product or brand might swell the manufacturer's chest, but it bores the pants off everyone else (ask yourself how long you could listen to a man in a pub extolling the virtues of a recent purchase). Boasting is seriously naff; telling people you're the best (or the most popular) is something else.

Because consumers have learned to doubt, they will accept very little on limited evidence. Your argument requires corroboration, your promise requires demonstration and your proposition requires proof. In short (**Proposition No. 21**): **Miracles must appear credible**.[7]

7   As to whether you choose emotional imagery or rational argument is up to you — and how precariously you're perched on the S-curve.

# STAY ON YOUR TOES

### Proposition No. 17

*Nobody counts the amount of ads you run; they just remember the impression you make.*

### Proposition No. 18

*Uninspired mediocrity is invisible.*

### Proposition No. 19

*Haemorrhoids are a pain in the neck.*

### Proposition No. 20

*To ensure consistency, young brand managers must be kept in line.*

### Proposition No. 21

*Miracles must appear credible.*

# STEP 5: READINGS FROM THE PROPHETS

I t's not unknown for religions to use a medium as the mouth-piece of the spirit world. In advertising, the medium has the power to dictate the shape development of creativity.

The late Marshall ('The medium is the message') McLuhan, a media guru and one of the 20th century's savviest prophets, surveyed the effects of successive media developments and declared that the pattern was essentially cannibalistic. In his view, new media do not replace the old media; they simply consume the body of the old.[1]

In this century, early cinema[2] began by feasting on the theatre's dramatic plots and the music hall's vaudeville routines.[3] Radio made extensive use of music-hall comedians, old plays and gramophone records (previously played only at home). Television has always subsisted on a diet of old movies and an up-to-date version of newsreels. Even the proliferating new TV channels put out a diet of old TV series. And so on, and so on.

McLuhan noted a human trait regarding acceptance of new ideas: that revolutionary new technological advances could only be comprehended in the context of what they replaced. For instance, the automobile was originally a *horse-less carriage*; early aircraft were called *flying machines*; the radio was once the *wireless*; silent movies metamorphosed into *talking pictures*. Long memories will also recall that the computer used to be called the *electronic brain*.

1   Not unlike new religions, which plunder the choicest morsels of the superseded religion and incorporate them into their beliefs.

2   Cinema's earliest viewing arenas were disused roller-skating rinks, a discarded Edwardian fad.

3   In the high days of radio, the US had a show featuring Charlie McCarthy, and the UK (on the BBC) had Archie Andrews. Both were ventriloquists' dummies. On *radio*.

Not only does this perception highlight a depressing lack of vision among humankind, it also demonstrates that most people are looking backwards over their shoulders when they should be looking ahead. It has a hobbling effect on any future development, not unlike trying to drive forwards using nothing but your rear-view mirror.

Cue for an historical overview (and an immediate apology). I am the first to admit that the following perspectives on advertising history are very Anglophonically biased and mainly US-centred. Sorry, but that's the way it is.

## BLOTTING YOUR COPY

Towards the end of the 19th century, standards of literacy among the masses began to improve and, together with the invention of the high-speed rotary press, they brought about the invention of the modern advertising agency. Suddenly newspapers and periodicals were being eagerly bought by a whole new class of consumer and the press assumed media dominance over the poster. Until then, publicity had been mainly visual and would have involved hand-painted billboards and lithographed posters.

In design terms, there were some devastating examples of high art,[4] but the persuasion quotient was mostly primitive Caveman stuff: logo and pack and sometimes even a snappy slogan. Hardly the raw bricks of brand building.

4  Notably Henri de Toulouse-Lautrec's brilliant lithographs and Alphonse Mucha's sinuous glamour girls.

In accordance with McLuhan's immutable law, early press ads set the engravers to work copying posters, but in monochrome. The important advantage of colour had to be sacrificed. It took an anonymous wordsmith to show that glittering words of praise can more than compensate for absence of colour. Modern copy-writing was born.

And it was through an astonishing development in electronics that the copywriter was raised from cub to king. Radio, the hottest new medium on the block, had no need of the time-honoured services of the illustrator, the engraver, lettering artists and the typographer. In radio, the writer ruled supreme. And radio was the most powerful and persuasive medium in the world, more intrusive and more personal than newspapers.

You could listen while you worked. And, where literacy levels were still low, you could enjoy radio without having the ability to read. With the added benefit of colourful voices, drama, sound effects and music, radio entertained. And it had a profound effect on the appearance of press and magazine advertising.

Contemplate these examples, all clipped out of the same November 1939 issue of the popular US women's magazine, the *Ladies' Home Journal.*

Ladies' Home Journal, US 1939

Ladies' Home Journal, US 1939

Nearly every ad in the magazine is presented in quasi-comic strip form. It could be seen as a patronizing gesture to the semi-illiterate, but hardly in the *Ladies' Home Journal*, a medium renowned for its features and fiction. No, the conversations between two housewives in a kitchen were lifted from performances in radio commercials. The comic strip format dictated the direction of the reader's gaze and unfolded the tale.

Of course, with the massive benefit of hindsight, we can now see that these ads were all prototype storyboards predicting the development of an audiovisual advertising medium, almost as though Madison Avenue were willing television into existence.

## THE SECRET LIFE OF BRAND X

Radio ruled as the dominant medium until after World War II, and when media dominance shifted inexorably towards television, agencies adhering to McLuhan's law persisted in using the new medium as radio plus pictures. It was only in product demonstration that the new medium developed an individual voice. And poor old 'Brand X', the eternal runner-up, became a television legend.[5]

As TV hit its stride, agencies hastily assembled slick formulas: apart from the usual celebrity endorsements, the world was introduced to dancing packs, white[6] knights, white tornadoes and much cheap animation. The word 'gimmick' became familiar. And even more familiar were the two women in a kitchen, who have hung on in there to this very day. The *Ladies' Home Journal* predictions were deadly accurate.

**5** Bizarrely, some guy actually registered and tried to market Brand X *as a legitimate brand*, on the grounds that it received more publicity than any single brand consumers could buy.

**6** TV, being only in black and white, cast all good things as white and all the bad ones as black.

In the US economy, prosperity was hitting the throttle, and memories of wartime rationing and shortages were being left behind. Materialism was replacing patriotism as the newest, most fashionable religion. Everybody wanted everything, and advertisers were in clover. Relishing success in times of plenty, the agencies were convinced that they had struck the right formula and the tone of US advertising became overheated and overhyped.

And a new term slipped into the vocabulary. 'Hard sell' described marketing in the macho mould, with no room for wimps. The product had to be promoted, stage front, as hero, with ads crammed full of an unremitting spiel.

## SELL HARD, SELL SOFT

This remorseless pitch left little room for the discriminating consumer, let alone the mouse. For during these Eisenhower boom years, new groups of consumers were being overlooked or ignored by the advertisers. Indeed, Madison Avenue had barely noticed the evolution of a new class of consumer, immune to the effects of the hard sell.

But, at the same time, certain small cults in New York were questioning orthodox dogma, reviewing practice, and planning the undermining of the unremittingly positive upbeatness in American advertising.

### DAVID OGILVY AND THE ART OF UNDERSTATEMENT

David Ogilvy was a remittance man excluded from the London advertising community by his brother Francis, who didn't want him truffling about on his patch. The young Ogilvy was

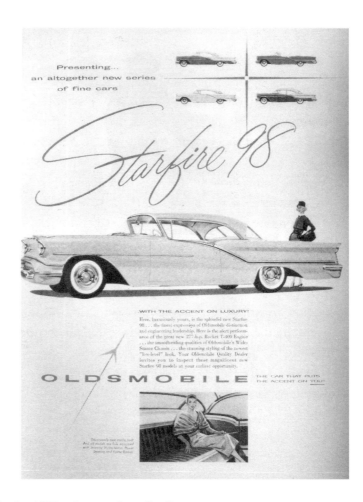

*In the 1950s, this was the soft sell* (© Graphic–Sha Publishing Company Ltd, Tokyo)

despatched to Manhattan and, on arrival, immediately identified a substantial congregation bypassed, or ill-addressed, by conventional agencies. It was the 'emergent gentry', the new rich who wanted guidance regarding behaviour, appearance, consumption and the rest.

"At 60 miles an hour the loudest noise in this
new Rolls-Royce comes from the electric clock"

What _makes_ Rolls-Royce the best car in the world? "There is really no magic about it —
it is merely patient attention to detail," says an eminent Rolls-Royce engineer.

Special showing of the Rolls-Royce and Bentley at Salter Automotive Imports, Inc., 9009 Carnegie Ave., tomorrow through April 26.

*Soft sell, Ogilvy style*

Ogilvy applied English (or, in his case, Scottish) snobbery and wrote[7] prose that, while spare, dripped with aristocratic understatement.

*At 60 miles an hour, the loudest noise in this new Rolls-Royce comes from the electric clock.[8]*

**7** OK, you anoraks, just testing. I know he didn't actually write the headline but purloined it from some upmarket motoring journal review.

**8** It might be apocryphal, but who cares? Note the response of the R-R executive who, on reading the ad, said: 'We must do something about that damned clock.'

In concentrating on the Rolls-Royce heritage, personality and superiority, Ogilvy, an artful copywriter and even better salesman, diffidently invited the consumer to make the brand's acquaintance. Stylistically cool, the arguments are confident and understated, with British upper-class restraint.

Previously 'soft-selling' was limited to the 'Starfire 98' approach: dripping with ersatz glamour. But this was a new kind of soft sell. The ad's low-temperature elegance and politeness knocked the American advertising business sideways and became the template for a new kind of *up*-marketing.

## THE RADICAL *CHUTZPAH* REVOLUTION

Meanwhile, in another corner of town on West 42nd Street, the ad agency of Doyle Dane Bernbach was fusing art directors of Italian and German origin with Jewish copywriters, to create a different kind of result. Bill Bernbach (the man who alerted the world to the fact that 85 per cent of all advertisements are never noticed) had identified yet another new market: an 'emergent intelligentsia', and discovered how to address it.

Urban and college-educated, the emergent intelligentsia comprised the children of hard-working immigrants and was becoming well-installed in academic life, the media and the professions. The emergent intelligentsia was not yet rich, but it was getting there. And on the way it was appreciating art and enjoying good music, literature and food. It was also sampling imported wines and contemplating trips to Europe.

The emergent intelligentsia stood beyond the transparent hucksterism of Madison Avenue, hard sell anathema aimed at the great unwashed. The emergent intelligentsia required a new mode of address: appealing to urban sophistication, cosmopolitan humour and a sense of style. And so Doyle Dane Bernbach invented the style: graphically austere, indebted to the Weimar Republic's influential Bauhaus,[9] married to witty, ironic, and often impolite copy.

Their ads were cheeky, funny and persuasive, the very embodiment of *chutzpah.*[10] For example:

*Presenting America's slowest fastback.*

*There are some new cars around with very streamlined roofs.*

*But they are not Volkswagens.*

*They are called fastbacks, and some of them are named after fish.*

*You can tell them from Volkswagens because a VW won't go over 72 mph. (Even though the speedometer shows a wildly optimistic top speed of 90.)*

*So you can easily break almost any speed law in the country in a VW.*

*And you can also cruise right past gas stations, repair shops and tire stores.*

*The VW engine may not be the fastest, but it's among the most advanced. It's made of magnesium alloy (one step better than aluminium). And it's so well machined you may never add oil between changes.*

9   Closed down by that graphic designer Adolf Hitler.

10   You want subtlety? I'll give you subtlety. Note that the VW logo on the ad, not very large, has been further reduced in strength by a half-line tone. It might reduce the visual strength. It does not reduce the power. Anyway, the car remains the single strongest recognition symbol.

**Presenting America's slowest fastback.**

*The VW engine is cooled by air, so it can never freeze up or boil over.*

*It won't have anything to do with water.*

*So we saw no reason to name it after a fish.[11]*

Now that's half a hemisphere away from *'Starfire 98, with the accent on luxury…'*.[12] And a textbook example of how to start a successful cult. (PS: over 40 years after excitedly tearing this ad out of *Esquire* magazine, I'm still knocked out about the fish joke.)

For the first time in American advertising, a shimmer of sophisticated wit. Doyle Dane's media department sought influential spaces and colonized that influential temple of suave urbanity, the *New Yorker* magazine. For the first time, there were ads that were able to hold their own against the elegant editorial

11  The creatives, when confronted with the original VW brief, rubbed their chins and said: *'You mean we've got to sell a Nazi car in a Jewish town?'*

12  And, if I may be permitted to enter a personal note, it's the sort of thing that some of us impressionable youngsters at the time thought pretty radical stuff.

and cerebral cartoons.[13] Clarity, hand-in-hand with brilliant new creativity in advertising, ruled.

Both schools junked the extraneous matter (the badges of *Good Housekeeping*, the logos, the exhortations to watch the sponsored TV show, etc, etc) that cluttered the communications of the day. And by adapting classic principles and simplicity (less is more, but God is in the details[14]), they conquered the media, attracted new talent to the business and ushered in a Golden Age.

I do not exaggerate, because this was indeed an age of miracles.

## Would you like to send an Avis button to your son at college?

We try harder.

Or to the man who installed your dishwasher? Or to the laundry that doesn't replace the buttons on your shirts?

It might wake up somebody you know. The way it did us.

The button jacked us up. It reminded us we were only No. 2 in rent a cars. With a lot more to do than just hand you a car like a lively new Ford.

We had to try harder to keep you coming back. All of us.

The girls at the counters, the men who fill up the gas tanks, the mechanics, the president back at the office. We're still only No.2. But we're inching up.

Pick up a button at any Avis counter. If the slogan doesn't work, turn it over. Try the pin.

*Sharp to the last line*

13 'An advertisement's greatest competition is not other advertisements, but the editor of the journal in which the ad is placed,' insisted the late Stanhope Shelton, creative director of Mather & Crowther and one of the great mentors of my copywriting apprenticeship.

14 Anybody can recite the first bit in praise of minimalism, but they never remember the second half, wherein lies the sting.

15   A veteran US adman once professed himself bemused about the success of the Polaroid camera, until it was pointed out that US legislation prohibited the sending of pornographic material through the mail. And most photo processing was sent by post.

It's worth noting that porn is quickest to embrace (if that's the right word) technological developments. We can guess that no sooner had Gutenberg invented moveable type, than someone in the next room was setting '…and her breasts were like melons'.

No sooner had Daguerre developed a photographic print of a silver teaspoon than someone in the next room was persuading a model to '… *drop 'em*'. And look what happened with film, video and the Internet.

16   There was a fad for wearing lapel buttons. One popular button read: '*Dress British. Think Yiddish*'.

Apart from selling a noisy small car (regardless of origin) in a gas-guzzling market, Doyle Dane Bernbach made a car-rental company interesting (Avis), turned a premium Scotch into a best seller (Chivas Regal), and launched one of the technological icons of the era (the self-processing Polaroid camera[15]). Confident that the Polaroid contained its own creativity, DDB allowed the product to announce its own miracles in a campaign refreshingly clear of starbursts and hype.

They didn't do it once: they did it over and over again. It was a time of iconoclasm and they ignited a Reformation. In the hands of experts, the new techniques were shown to be efficient and their sparks ignited fresh thinking and new careers all over the world.

Advertising had undergone a major creative shift.[16] And a new orthodoxy was in the process of revealing itself. Birth, I'd call it.

## TOMORROW BEGINS HERE

*Birth.* And that locates its position in the relentless pattern of the life cycle: gestation, birth, puberty, maturity, decay, death, rebirth. Everything on earth (and beyond) is subject to the immutable laws of the life cycle, whether you're Albert Einstein or a banana palm.

*Birth? Growth? Death?* All are the very stuff of religion, which finds its way into every passage rite (circumcision, christening, confirmation, marriage, funeral). The life cycle curve can be applied to fads, fashions, cultural movements, governments and human relationships. Even the state of advertising creativity.

As you'll discover, in close cahoots with the S-curve it can reduce your problems too.

However, new media evolve as you read, and all the rules will change. For instance – are you ready for this?:

*'The hottest 3D virtual reality sex online,' boasts Hot & Heavy, a Dutch cybersex emporium. 'Use your mouse to move the hottest girls/couple in 3D. Latest Quick-Time VR Technology!' Using the latest software, which allows computer users to move around and manipulate objects in 3D, such sites are pushing the edges of what's possible for Net and CD ROM users who seek liaisons with digitized cyberbabes and cyberstuds. Computer users can also experience 3D sex CD ROMs.*

*All these activities are loosely termed 'VR' or 'cybersex'. But they pale into insignificance in comparison with the likely future VR experience, say programmers. Aficionados of VR erotica are waiting for 'teledildonics', the ability to interact not just visually but through touch with a 3D computerized playmate.*

*Already the technology exists to create a 3D replica of a live model, which could be explicitly animated. Using the techniques already used in film, animators could place a woman (or a man, presumably) on a rotating platform and scan her with a laser. As her body rotates, the laser measures the distance to points on the body in vertical slices, creating a 'ring of technology' as one Los Angeles animator puts it. The points are then connected, to create a frame that mirrors the woman's body. Then, motion sensors could be placed on the model to capture specific movements. Add skin and texture to the model and you would have a virtual clone. Such a model could respond to computer or voice commands: 'You could tell her to do anything you want,' says one Hollywood film industry engineer.*

*In the longer term – perhaps a decade away – he predicts the ability to get and give virtual satisfaction through sensory interactivity. Using a helmet-like device, which enables a user to see into a computer-generated world, and a dataglove that receives and transmits the sensation of touch, a person can already enter an interactive digital world. A research team in Germany has produced a prototype full-body sensory suit for clumsy sex. The technology is clumsy now, but that's predicted to change.*

*'The Blade Runner-type sex toy is in the future,' says the engineer. But 'it's not a question of whether or not it's going to get here; it's when'.[17]*

17    *Guardian Online* 14 May 1998. Quoted in full.

When? Soon. A threat? Only if you haven't been paying attention so far. For there is a method of handling the threat. And it was predicted as long ago as 1955, before I had ever even considered advertising as a career.

I was appraised of both problem and solution when I was curled up inside a large chintzy armchair, chomping on an apple while glued to a science fiction novel by Shepherd Mead, the man who wrote *How to Succeed in Business Without Really Trying*. In his novel, *The Big Ball Of Wax*,[18] he predicts fresh media developments that threaten conventional thinking, with disaster of continental-drift proportions.

18    Mayflower Science Fiction 1962 (first published 1955).

MAYFLOWER SCI-FI

*The* BIG BALL *of* WAX

shepherd mead

Sometime in the early 1990s,[19] the sales of a brand plummet to zilch in a mid-West US city. The brand owner is concerned and a young account manager from the agency is dispatched to discover the cause. The cause is simple: no one in that mid-West US city is watching TV (and thus the brand's ads) any more. Why? Because they're all attending services of a new religious cult in the local cinema.

Our young hero buys a ticket and is strapped into one of rows and rows of identical dentist's chairs, each topped with an electronic headset, replacing the conventional cinema seats. Suddenly, from the freshly parted curtains on the stage, a most beautiful priestess hoves into view, deep of cleavage and heady of scent. She advances, making unequivocal advances to him while begging donations to the church.

Our hero extricates himself from the chair and notices that there is no one on stage. Snooping behind the scenes, he finds a prototype new style of videotape machine playing to all the dentist chair headsets. And he meets two young men, both brilliant electronic engineers, who have developed techniques for recording (and playing back) all the remaining senses unrecorded: touch, smell, taste.

The young man returns to New York headquarters full of gloom about how this religion will kill TV nationally, and therefore the entire advertising business. The agency, too, is sunk in gloom – until the creative director arrives on the rooftop by helicopter and shows them to the new boardroom, secretly constructed with a dentist's chair for each member of the board.

They are all wired in and each finds himself suddenly clothed in rags, crawling across Death Valley, about 130° in the shade. Except there's no shade. After about ten minutes of knee-grinding torture, the shadow of a sumptuous blonde model hoves into view, slowly and seductively, and pours a bottle of ice-cold beer into a long, frosted glass.

The sound of pouring is heavily amplified as the blonde leans forward and offers the crawling executive a long, deep drink.

And *CUT.*

The board is faced by the smiling creative director who says '... *and that, gentlemen, is how we're going to treat the new medium'.*

With a single hoarse voice, the entire board is croaking for beer.

When virtual reality arrives (and it's around the corner), agencies will strive to make the medium perform on behalf of their clients' brands. On the assumption that the creative talent is present, the industry shouldn't take long to find ways through or over the new brick wall.

But I suspect that for a time the new medium will be treated like the old media, and opportunities for progress and profit will be lost. At least until McLuhan's law is obeyed. When the new medium has digested the old, it's time for creativity to begin.

## A THOUGHT AT TWILIGHT

No propositions to revise. But an awful lot to remember. And contemplate.

# STEP 6: THE QUEST FOR GOODNESS

It must have come to your ears (mainly because it's one of those advertising truisms muttered towards the end of the evening in darkened bars) that clients eventually wind up with the agencies they deserve (and vice versa). But remember this: all the power rests with the clients. As God's representatives, they are the paymasters. They choose the agencies. They hire. And they fire.

Strange, then, that all too frequently and for all the right reasons, clients make the wrong choice.[1]

A senior food client once presented a neat analogy for the different agencies on offer. 'Ordinary agencies,' he said, 'are like faded restaurants: so-so food with polite waiters. Whereas, in 'creative' agencies, the kitchen is brilliant, but the waiters are inclined to be stroppy.' Some clients put up with stroppy (read 'passionate') waiters for decent nosh. Others insist on decent manners (read 'plenty of respect and restraint, but no passion') all the time, but then they were probably brought up on lousy food.

In the end, time and events decide whether or not a choice is flawed (chastening motto: time waits for no brand), but even then, if the agency–client relationship is not based on trust and mutual respect, it is doomed anyway. For when a client loses faith in its agency, then the product of the alliance will be sterile.

In the cause of greater advertising efficiency, let's establish this line of argument: 'Ultimately, good advertising is more beneficial

[1] For some remote reason, usually blamed on 'chemistry'. What's wrong with geography or history? I ask.

**2** International soft drink company at pre-production meeting for commercial to be shot on a Florida beach. Ten years after the event, they had learned of Women's Lib. and announced: *'All girls in this commercial will be wearing bras.' 'Where?'* I asked, *'underneath or above their bikini tops?'*

**3** Inexplicably, my publishers (and their libel lawyers) refuse to allow me to name names. But a flick through the back issues of *Campaign* will reveal those clients that appointed Bartle Bogle Hegarty (because they were the hottest agency in town) and then dropped them because they wouldn't descend to Caveman tactics.

**4** Forget love–hate, these are hate–hate relationships, particularly if they're (a) international and (b) imposed from the company's head office in another country.

to the bottom line than bad advertising.' I'm profoundly aware that the most inaudible bat-squeak of dissent with the previous sentence would put one in league with those against motherhood, apple pie and the flag, and so perhaps it would be wiser to examine the meaning of 'good' as applied to advertising. And it follows that the path leads naturally to an investigation of the description 'good' in the cases of agencies and clients.

Let's start with clients.

## BAD CLIENTS

Time after time, history shows that nasty dictatorial clients with control freak tendencies[2] stay with agencies they can bully.[3] These relationships[4] are seldom happy because the agencies, in turn, are forced to apply bullying tactics towards the consumer. And, like everyone else, most consumers resent bullying and stop patronizing the brand. History also reveals that agencies hobbled by their clients' prejudices[5] are less able to retain a keen creative edge, and begin to slip down the agency league.[6]

## GOOD CLIENTS

In my opinion good clients believe in exceptional advertising talent. They are aware that such talent possesses an ability to empathize with their consumers by producing exciting stimuli.[7]

Good clients such as Sony, Volkswagen, Whitbread, Diageo[8] and Volvo have good advertising because it is part of their corporate culture. They actively plan for it because they desire it. And they desire it because experience has shown them that good advertising has been more beneficial to their bottom lines than bad advertising.

For what it's worth, my four-attributes-that-make-a-Good-Client list follows:

1.  *communicative*: sharing their plans and research;

2.  *stimulating and encouraging*: actually desiring and appreciating exciting communication;

3.  *receptive*: knowing when they're on to something positive and productive;

4.  *courageous*: refusing to junk a promising scheme to satisfy cautious critics.

*A PAIR OF PARABLES*

First, an instructive parable about the values of being communicative.

Time: late 80s. The agency for which I am working presents a new TV campaign to a large fast food client. Because the product is chicken, the creative team on the business has invented a campaign with an animated fox (resident chicken expert) as the presenter. Campaign is sold, ads are made, and they are then run in a test market. Campaign scores as a great success.

US management turns up to inspect commercial. 'What's with the fox? We don't want to associate our product with vermin.' Fox campaign is axed.

5   For obvious reasons, agencies beset by dictatorial clients haemorrhage creative talent. A paucity of creative talent means no decent ads. No decent ads means unsuccessful clients. Clients lacking success fire their agencies. Relegation looms.

6   Standard adbiz solution: go out and buy a new, bright agency.

7   Occasionally bad clients are given good advertising, but they don't hang on to it for long. It flies in the face of their dogma, and sooner or later some poor sucker has to pay.

8   The result of the merger between Guinness and International Distillers & Vintners. I can't speak for Guinness, but IDV were always excellent clients.

Ripple dissolve as time races on a few years.

Same client has requested pitch from a different agency and turns up to view result. Ads are shown and agency patiently awaits response. 'Oh shit,' exclaims the client management in mild consternation. 'It's another fox.' Effectively it's an automatic verbal thumbs-down.

'What do you mean *another* fox?' asks the perplexed agency. Blushing and farting on the client side. 'Oh well, we once had a fox but we didn't like it,' they stammer in response. In an attempt to subjugate their anger and confusion, the agency clears its collective throat and states: '(a) You never mentioned that to us, either in the brief or conversation; and (b) there wasn't a single commercial featuring a fox anywhere on your archive reel.'

'Didn't we mention it?' replies the client, examining its corporate nails. 'Oh dear, maybe not. But it's only because we didn't like the old campaign. We removed it from the reel and vowed never to discuss it again.'

Parable two serves as an antidote concerning a client being stimulating, encouraging, receptive and courageous.

In June 1972, I joined an agency called the Kirkwood Company, which had a large portfolio of liquor brands. On my first day, account director Gordon Medcalf put his head around the door and asked if I could scribble a cinema script for him because he had a meeting due and no work to show.

'What's the brand?' I asked.

'It's called Vladivar Vodka,' he replied.

'Where does it come from?' I asked.

'Warrington,' he replied.

Fortunately for Gordon, the client, the agency *and* my career, I had grown up in Muizenberg, a seaside suburb of Cape Town, surrounded by Russian Jewish immigrants. Simple mimicry told me that they would pronounce Warrington with a 'V' sound. '*Vladivar Wodka from Varrington.*' It even sounded funny.[9]

Greenalls, who owned the brand,[10] were brewers, vintners and distillers and owned most of the pubs in the north-west of England. They'd entered into a contra-deal with Bass Charrington Vintners (Kirkwood's client), which involved replacing Smirnoff by putting Vladivar Vodka on optic behind the bar in every Bass pub.

But, because Smirnoff was the most fashionable and popular vodka brand in the UK, Bass Charrington Vintners adopted a marketing tactic of trying to persuade consumers not to refuse, as they often did, the brand on optic in favour of Smirnoff. In other words, the role of the cinema ads (Kirkwood's media department had decided that cinema was the place to catch the target market and that two commercials were required) was to buy a little recognition, and non-rejection, for a totally unknown brand.

**9** When my sister Tamara saw the commercial, she commented, quite accurately, 'Those aren't Russians. That's the Muizenberg synagogue committee.'

**10** It was subsequently sold to another company.

I wrote the entire campaign[11] that very day and, a week later, accompanied Gordon to Warrington. When we presented the storyboard to David Kopp, the marketing director, he laughed. He tugged me into a second office, and I presented it to his superior, who guffawed. They called in a few other members of the salesforce who happened to be lolling about the offices, and that constituted the sales conference. They fell about uncontrollably. The campaign was sold.

Kopp was a maverick genius with a talent for PR. After learning that Russian delegates walked out of the Cannes screening of the commercial, he made sure that not only was an official Russian trade delegation invited to the trade screening, but that the press were also tipped off. As expected, the Russians simulated a rapid attack of high dudgeon and stalked out.[12] That very night, the commercials were screened on BBC1's Nine O'Clock News.

When David spotted that a maverick entrepreneur was offering ads on the sides of cows grazing along the railway line to Brighton, everyone in conventional media scoffed at the idea. Kopp bought them all for Vladivar, and the brand featured on front pages in newspapers all over the world.

A tiny budget stretched by hard work grabbed a sizeable chunk of Smirnoff's market. Vladivar had become a cult brand.

How much of a cult I discovered for myself one night at a serious movie buff's cinema in Islington. I was present when a Vladivar commercial was shown and wondered at the curious whispered reaction among the audience until I recognized that they were reciting the dialogue along with the actors.

Curiously, Bass Charrington Vintners, stuffed to the gills with real gents in school ties, were decidedly sniffy about the whole business. 'An aberration,' they harrumphed. 'Totally unorthodox. Not the proper way to sell spirits.' Of course, had they paid heed to Helen Keller, they would have learned that 'this year's heresy becomes next year's orthodoxy'. And so it did.

Digging a little deeper into the qualities of good clients, here follows a tale of receptivity.

At the end of the 1980s, I was executive creative director[13] of a large international advertising agency called Wasey Campbell-Ewald.[14] Wasey's had held on to the Goodyear tyre account since the agency opened its London office as Erwin Wasey Rathrauff and Ryan[15] as long ago as 1919. Goodyear, the world's largest tyre company, was also the biggest name in Formula One racing tyres, and for decades its advertising slogan was 'Choice of Champions'.

For almost equally as long a time, Goodyear's international advertising had emerged from Akron, Ohio, an industrial city constructed on rubber, but not an epicentre of communications sophistication. It was a cosy arrangement. The international ad manager would go to New York and collect the writer, and they'd settle in London for a while and write the new international campaign based on Formula One's star drivers[16] and how Goodyear helped them negotiate rain-sodden tracks. The executive creative

13  No, I do not know the difference between executive and non-executive creative directors.

14  Yes, I know it's a silly name. No, it's not as silly as the long-dead Horniblow Cox-Freeman or the US firm Larsen, Colby, Koralek, a division of Levene, Huntley, Schmidt and Beaver. The British Duckworth, Finn, Grubb and Weaver takes a lot of beating too.

15  You wanted more silly names?

16  Suss the integral flaw? Motor racing's high-risk factor means that commercials needed continuous re-editing.

director of the London office was never involved, except to be wheeled out occasionally to shake the hand of a new immensely tall man with silver hair from the mid-West.

Cosy, but out of touch. In focus groups, European consumers were saying that ordinary car tyres were totally unlike racing tyres and the comparison was irrelevant.[17]

Suddenly, the picture changes. New international executive, but neither tall, nor with silver hair. Jack Sardas is a tough, wiry individual who runs eight miles daily before breakfast. He turns up at an annual presentation in London and wants to know why the agency is taking the money and running. The agency team, unused to discordant meetings, is nonplussed and serves a halting argument defending the status quo. Sardas returns a crushing ultimatum that, if the agency doesn't clean up its act in two weeks and present a new campaign, the agency is fired.

There are key phrases that galvanize agency managements. One is *'increased billing'*. Another is *'fired'*. The ad team is changed. The executive creative director is informed. Meanwhile, tremors run through the New York office. 'Jeez, guys, if London loses the business, we'll lose it in 42 offices around the world.'

Another galvanizing term is 'lose'. New York decides to dispatch its top talent from Detroit. The London agency office manager is losing hair trying to find enough free desks for mid-Westerners jetting in at vast cost.

**17** Marketing gurus will tell you that (a) because of improved techniques of manufacture, new tyres now last over three years; (b) fleet cars, which account for most new car registrations, are usually kept for a maximum of three years; (c) very few people specify the tyres on new cars; and (d) most people replace the make of tyre already on the car with the same make. Therefore, it would seem, that ads for new tyres will only really start to work after three years. Curious.

*THE BRAND*

Let's pause to discuss the brand itself. As usual, the giant thumbnail of irony hovers above the enterprise: as one branch of the client is ditching Grand Prix motor racing as an advertising theme, another has called the new tyre brand the Goodyear Grand Prix 'X'.

Road research on the tyre shows that it scored better than the competition in a whole string of tests. But there are so many improvements that it is very difficult to shoehorn them into a single commercial, as requested by the brief.

'If it's better than the others in so many ways, can we say that this is the best tyre in the world?' I ask the international ad manager.

Humming and hawing. 'Maybe,' comes the answer.

'Well then, if it's the best tyre in the world, it must be the *safest* tyre in the world,' I suggest.

Less humming and more heavy aspiration. 'You can't say that.'

'No,' I reply, 'yet it's exactly what the consumer wishes to hear. You're right, you can't say it, but someone else can. If you find the right presenter, it enables you to make a series of commercials demonstrating how the Grand Prix X is superior to the competition, each commercial extolling one facet – like road-holding in the wet, or braking, or mileage.'

'Yeah,' says the mid-West. 'But who's the presenter?' The air in my office grows cold. Now, I cannot testify to the fact, but that supernatural chill must have occurred at the nanosecond when my muse decided to look in for a chat. Without ever knowing what prompted me, I add, 'Someone like Sir Robert Mark could,' surrendering to some cosmic autopilot.

'Who's *he*?' ask the mystified mid-Westerners present.

Patiently I explain about the man, recently retired, known as Mr Clean of Scotland Yard, the man who cracked the Spaghetti House and Balcombe Street sieges.

'Oh,' they exclaim. 'Sort of like a British J Edgar Hoover? How do we get him?'

'By explaining the tyres' safety margins as a huge improvement in road safety.'

I brief the creative team, and Roger Beattie writes the clinching line for Sir Robert: '*I believe it's a serious contribution to road safety.*'

Our lucky stars are on maximum dazzle. On retirement from the Met., Sir Robert is asked to become president of a police charity. When he hears about the opportunity of appearing in commercials, he accepts on condition he is allowed to donate his entire fee to the fund.

Sardas likes the new campaign and stays the threat of execution. The international advertising manager, who had never liked the solution (deeply concerned by words like 'safety'), comes round to the idea after he is awarded an initialled parking space at the Akron head office car park.

After the campaign is rather spectacularly launched, he drops in on our Brazilian office. Over a cup of coffee with the creative director he says, 'You know, you guys should do a campaign like the Limeys. Their Lord Mark campaign is going gangbusters.'

The Brazilian creative director looks him square in the eye and says: *'And where do you expect us to find an honest cop in Brazil?'*

Here's an arresting sidelight to the Goodyear story.

Everything had to be under the tightest wraps. Whereas all the first batch of commercials were shot on Goodyear's own Texan test track, we wanted the launch commercial to be shot on a motorway bridge in England. On a filthy wet day, Sir Robert stood with his elbow on the parapet, cars with headlamps ablaze forming ribbons behind him, as he started to say his lines: *'I have never allowed my name to be used in advertising before, but when I heard about…'*.

Seconds before the director signals for action, a motorway police car slides to a halt on the damp bridge among the detritus of camera cases, lights, generators and the paraphernalia of filming. Policeman climbs out, flexes his muscles and asks to speak to man in charge. Production company producer walks over: 'Can I help you, Officer?'

'Did you arrange for permission to do all this?'

'Yes. We have town and county police permission.'

'Ah,' says copper, rearranging his triceps, 'but do you have *motorway* police permiss...'

At that precise second, the giant ten-kilowatt film lights switch on to cut through the drizzly gloom with an intense glare. The policeman's attention is diverted. 'Er, is that who I think it is?' he asks, a new tremor disturbing the confidence of his delivery.

'Yes,' answers the producer without any show of emotion.

'Well, I'll be off then,' says the copper, departing in the car and accelerating almost dangerously.

Incidentally, like Vladivar, the commercials were previewed on the UK's TV news.

## THE LURKING MORAL

Moral? The moral is **Proposition No. 22: Nothing is for nothing**.

By its very nature, advertising is a very public activity and extremely competitive in its nature. You can only take the money and run for so long before someone finds you out. When honesty is unwelcome, the resulting advertising is going to be unhealthy for the brand and the client. The trouble is that, while good clients have every right to expect their agencies to be honestly objective, there are a number of snags.

Many clients, particularly those who are actually involved in the manufacture of the product themselves, become too closely involved with the brand to be anything but subjective. It's understandable: if, say, the previous six weeks have been involved in long committee meetings about the precision machining of an aluminium grommet, then consideration of the aluminium grommet looms larger than the surveying of the overall picture. But even then, it doesn't make it statutory that the aluminium grommet should be included in the advertising: the epochal advertising for Volkswagen was born not in Germany but in the United States, many thousands of miles away; Chivas Regal advertising in Britain was fusty, while the brand's advertising broke all records in the States; in contrast, judging by its frequent appearances at international awards ceremonies for the past couple of decades, Levi's' advertising in Britain has been an improvement on anything produced in the States.

Honesty can be swamped in overclaim – not so much in copy overclaim but in unrealistic promises about the success a campaign can achieve. The more honest the brief, the tighter the campaign objectives, the more realistic the expectations, and the clearer the criteria for judging the creative work and its probable effect. *No brand, no advertising, no client can be dishonest for long and not be found out.*

These days, cover-ups are out of the question. Perrier, after a problem with pollution that could easily have buried the brand, adroitly managed their way out of catastrophe by being decisive and honest. Honesty requires confidence. And honesty requires bravery. So too does successful brand management. Good clients are brave and encourage their agencies to be original and bold.

Anything else is not worthy of consideration. Unoriginal, timid advertising is neutral and invisible. Invisible advertising, while causing no consternation in the boardroom, is actually a black hole that consumes money without trace. And nobody who wastes money is a hero.

Last word on honesty: good clients trust their agencies and expect the same trust in return. In fact, if an agency ever betrays a client's trust, it should be fired. And that is **Proposition No. 23: If an agency ever betrays a client's trust, it should be fired**.

# PROPOSITIONS FOR ENLIGHTENMENT

## Proposition No. 22

*Nothing is for nothing.*

## Proposition No. 23

*If an agency ever betrays a client's trust, it should be fired.*

# STEP 7: THE GOD AGENCY GUIDE

So there we are: the heavenly attributes of the good marketing director have been established. Now we can consider some related questions.

*Q:* Where is this paragon found?

*A:* In the more enlightened corporations that encourage creative thought.

Which leads to the next question:

*Q:* How do you find the more enlightened corporations?

*A:* By investigating the client lists of the more intelligent, more liberated ad agencies.

*More intelligent, more liberated agencies?* What are they? Who are they? Where are they? And how do you get them working for you?

## WHICH?

It was never intended that this book should be the client's Bible of agencies,[1] but they are worth a few words and a return trip to the past.

All agencies are shaped by two factors:

1  Now there's a good idea.

1. *The growth imperative*

Agencies are driven by a mantra that buzzes in every chief executive's brain: 'If we don't put on any new business, we're dead.' The more unsuccessful an agency, the greater the percentage of agency energy expended in chasing new business. And the greater the percentage of creative time spent in inventing new lures to tempt clients.

2. *History*

Not too long ago, there were agencies that dated from pre-World War II days, restricted by outworn dogma imposed by distant pontiffs.[2] There were others that functioned as the remote branch offices of a huge Vatican-like organization, established to service head office clients in foreign parts. Yet others were formed in more enlightened times, and still retain the imprint of a fiery, founding personality. And there were agencies, even younger, that succeeded by practising outrageous heresy, inverting the values of the established belief.

Their successes with clients varied and depended upon their abilities to interpret the reading of confessionals (research) and to convert them into stimuli that would tickle the public's appropriate G-spot. The pattern has never changed.

The older, larger agencies, sensitive to shareholder pressure, are prone to compromise any principles they might have had, and the work becomes more predictable and even duller. By dangling the lure of big bread, dull agencies are able to attract exciting creatives

**2**   After being toppled, one pontiff was seen leaving his office clutching an enormous portrait of himself, almost twice his size.

but, in an atmosphere of 'just do what the client wants', they are unable to persuade them to stay.

Agencies that cannot retain creative talent find themselves in trouble. Their inability to create exciting campaigns corresponds with their lack of success at gaining new clients. And, in the agency business, survival depends on gaining new business. A poor record has the effect of making shareholders feel very nervous.

Therefore the age-old system continues, with the older, richer agencies transfusing the smaller, livelier agencies into their lifeblood so as to stave off hardening arteries caused by a liflelong regime of excessive compromise. As a system, it falls into the sector labelled 'hit-or-miss'. In some cases, it has worked well; in others, the resulting culture clash has damned the entire enterprise almost before it has begun.

## ANYTHING TO DECLARE?

Clients hunting for new agencies always seem to arrive overladen with luggage. If opened and examined, the trunks would reveal a loose collection of key criteria, particularly the desire to be associated with an agency that:

◆ *has successful clients;*
◆ *has solved similar problems to ours;*
◆ *is big (or small);*
◆ *is sales-oriented;*
◆ *is research-led;*

- *is dedicated to planning;*
- *works through the line;*
- *is famous;*
- *has a sure-fire formula for success;*
- *will number us among their larger clients;*
- *and, very occasionally, is creative.*

'Creative' is one of those Humpty-Dumpty words. You can make it mean exactly what you choose it to mean. Everyone offers different definitions and even two creatives in a pub will disagree on the precise meaning of the word.

Years ago, I was part of a team making an agency credentials presentation to a very large corporation that we imagined was a prospective client. We showed that we had revitalized a traditionally conventional agency and that we were now producing fresh and exciting work (my definition of 'creative'). Missing the point completely, the deputy marketing director of the large corporation later complained that I had not presented a mnemonic or acronym to explain our approach to making ads (*his* definition of 'creative'.) We were not awarded any business.

Bernbach always warned clients to beware agencies who produce glib formulas to guarantee success. Often it's clear that more creativity oil has been burned inventing the formula than will ever go into your ads.

*THE USP*

Take, for example, Ted Bates and the Unique Selling Proposition (USP), invented by Rosser Reeves, a Batesian advertising huckster of mythic stature. Seeking a notion to arrest the attention of clients, he seized on the USP, which he defined as the brand's main point of differentiation from its competitors. Once uncovered, the USP would constitute the platform for all product promotion.

So far, so good. But what Reeves had done was simply to isolate a single strand of any worthwhile creative's approach to constructing an ad: locate and dramatize the product difference.

Reeves took it further and turned it into the keystone of Bates' philosophy, with an argument running along the lines: once research has helped us select the relevant USP (*'washes whiter'*, *'relieves indigestion in nine different ways'*, *'reaches parts other aspirins do not reach'*), we never let it go. Again, using research, we construct the most efficient ad around the USP and run it for ever, in tune with our belief that ads only start to work when they're boring you to distraction.

Reeves' notion was brilliant business, because it actually excluded the one variable in producing ads: creative talent. Because all the work could be done by researchers, creatives had been decreed unnecessary and were sidelined.

Bates and Reeves made great capital of the USP's pseudo-scientific basis[3] (never forget that the first book about modern

3   Reeves published a book called, unsurprisingly, *Reality in Advertising.*

advertising was Claude Hopkins' *Scientific Advertising*) and its primary audience seemed to be pharmaceutical manufacturers, makers of household cleaners and toiletry companies. Madison Avenue wags had it that you could tell the Bates commercial by the man in the white coat (those were the days when you could run a title: 'a doctor', 'a dentist', 'a scientist', making full use of stern but benign figures of authority).

The Bates USP approach concealed more cunning than first meets the eye. In running ads unchanged, sometimes for years, they could survive with fewer troublesome creatives who wanted to keep in tune with fashion. Fewer creatives also meant a smaller salary bill and broader margins. First rule of advertising: *if you ain't got something, knock it.*[4]

The USP was not without success in the early days of US TV, and the Bates agency grew famous and successful. People outside the agency attributed the success and fame to the three letters U, S and P, and suddenly, all over Madison Avenue, copycat admen were hunting acronyms to boost their fortune.

Inside agencies, account teams were searching for USPs as though they were the panacea to all of advertising's creative problems. They weren't. They were simply another promotional gimmick hyped to breaking point.

Here are some more.

Richard Cook's piece in *The Independent* on 18 May 1998 caught my eye. I read it and then read it again. You try:

**4**  For a very short while, I worked in London with an old Bates veteran. Heading for a food-client pitch, he instructed the account team to visit the client's factory and discover the product's protein content.

'Very important, protein is,' he said.

Account team returns and reports: 'Sorry, no protein.'

'In which case,' says the old Bates hand, 'the headline reads: 'LESS HARMFUL PROTEIN'.'

*... [creatives] got to keep irregular hours, grow all sorts of interesting facial hair and pay scant regard to personal hygiene. They were, you see, creative and mindful of the fact that the sober-suited business decisions were happening elsewhere in the agency. Their job was to create; others could handle the mundane things, such as presenting the idea to the client or planning the campaign.*

*But times change... and sometimes they do change for the better. 'The bright, forward-thinking creatives have realized that the circumstances have altered. In fact they have welcomed that change,' says xxxxxx, a partner in the recently started xxxxxx advertising agency that styles itself as the first holistic communications company.*

*'A new breed of creative has started to appear since the last recession,' he adds, 'in part because life post-recession has been a little less forgiving. A creative can't take liberties just for being creative any more.*

*'As a consequence, the misplaced arrogance of the past has had to go. For instance, creatives have to turn up for meetings on time and sober, which for many is a new concept.'*

*More important still has been the fact that the new creatives have recognized the opportunities that flexibility in working practices is allowing. While it may have been fun for them to spend days locked in their offices waiting for a moment of inspiration to strike, they can actually make a greater contribution to the creative process by working as part of a team. That way, they also have a better chance of seeing the work they produce make it before the public at large.*

This has 'USP' stamped all over it: an attempt at a new formula impress clients. It has about it that happy-clappy feeling of 'let's bury our differences and all work together to solve humanity's problems'. And the veiled threats about changing former restrictive working practices sounds like the venting of bloodlust at the Federation of Mill Owners' annual general conference. '*New breed of creative*'? That's agency-speak for '*realistic*', with intended subtext: '*We will obey your every instruction, Sir.*'

Sorry, it's yet another new agency trying to bait the hook with things the client wants to hear. Stuff and nonsense, of course. Agencies should be telling you what you need to know.

My friend Ed's ex-father-in-law (a genius who invented a revolutionary new form of film lighting in the forties that made his fortune) was invited to be a business consultant by a large Japanese watch-manufacturing company. When he stated his required fee, the watch executives recoiled in shock. 'Why, that's far too much,' they protested, after recovering their balance, adding 'after all, we know everything there is to know about making and selling watches.'

'Correct,' said Ed's ex-father-in-law. 'You know all about watches. I know about everything else.' He got the project.

You know all about your business. Agencies (should) know about everything else. They're not supposed to be specialists in soft drinks formulation or high-performance engines. But they are supposed to be specialists at getting people to want them.

If the anonymous agency making that desperate pitch only had experience of drunk creatives, then the work must have been terrible. Putting freshly sobered creatives into suits might make the work more saleable, but no better.

## How?

So, what are you seeking? Forget about your baggage and obscure references to chemistry, as though agencies contain some sort of pheromone that will attract you like a sex-starved moth. Please deny most of those criteria, because all the evidence (ie the agency you eventually appoint after your slog around town) is that they are a chimera, fanciful conceptions that exist only in your imagination.

Admit it: they have no bearing on reality. Because what you're really looking for is *hot*. Deep down inside, god-like creature that you might be, even you are affected by physical attraction. '*Hot*' is another word for '*sexy*', or '*charismatic*', or, as an earlier generation might have put it, '*glamorous*'. With ample reason, clients get the feeling that an agency's glamour might rub off onto their brand.

### Recognizing 'hot'

But how on earth do you recognize a really hot agency? Ignore the threatening crouch of Ferraris in the car park. Ignore the reception lobby papered with award certificates. Remember only these three things:

**First:** and most important, **The agency must have a cracking reel.**[5]

5 Proposition No. 24.

**Comment:** It's one thing to have clever ideas.

It's another to turn them into brilliant ads.

If the agency in question can perform that trick time after time, they have the mark of a great agency.

**Second:** **The agency will never present more than one campaign at a time.**[6]

6 Proposition No. 25.

**Comment:** Never trust an agency that presents a raft of campaigns while examining the pupils of your eyes to discover your favourite.

Able creative agencies present and recommend a single campaign. It is the fruit of their planning, ingenuity, originality and artistry.

If you think it is wrong, reject it. But be warned: disliking it because it is strange or unfamiliar is a flimsy excuse to junk the idea.

If you wanted the commonplace or the familiar, you should never have hired them in the first place.

Buying a campaign requires an element of bravery. Cowardly campaigns excite no one. Least of all consumers.

Displaying multiple campaigns is a sign of nervousness, indecision and lack of confidence in a creative solution.

An agency displaying multiple solutions is showing off:

*'Look how clever we are, We've invented three ways of solving the problem.'*

*Sorry, guys.*

And

*third:* **The agency has the guts to part company with clients on matters of deep principle.**[7]

7   Proposition No. 26.

***Comment:*** true creativity in the advertising business is about putting principles on the bottom line.

Agencies should be willing to split with clients who continuously reject their advice (as someone once said, *'Principles are only principles when they cost you money.'*).

But the job of finding a truly creative agency is complicated by the fact that too many agencies pose as creative.

Being creative is not about adopting a modish posture.

Being creative is not about striking the right brand of attitude.

Being creative is about being talented, intelligent, courageous and individual.

Being creative is about being different. Or as David Abbott once said, **'When everyone is zigging, you need to zag'**.[8]

8   Has to be Proposition No. 27.

Talented, intelligent, courageous, individual and different: it is difficult to be all five. Which, perhaps, accounts for the rarity of hot agencies.

Bearing in mind these three points (and four Propositions), there is a very simple route to recognizing a hot agency, which suffers the unfashionable disadvantage of being subjective.

First, you are urged to ignore the hype and the media massaging of ego.

Second, look around and see what advertising you actually notice. Make a note of the work that really affects you, the sort of stuff that makes you laugh, or cry, or part with loot. If you admire a new brand launch or the spectacular revival of a failing brand's fortune, then somebody, somewhere is doing something right. (By being predictive – rather than predictable – the work of hot agencies has a tendency to stand out. If it appears to be unfamiliar, wait. See if it is actually in tune with events about to unfold.)

Uncover the name of the agency.

If it is as good as the ads would indicate, it means that someone in the place has a keyhole (if not a direct line) to the future, and someone in the place really understands the market. However much agencies hype their skills and insights, that sort of expertise is rare. Anybody can read the past; it takes an oracle to divine the future. And all business exists in the future.

Find out the name of the agency and appoint them before your opposition does.

*THREE PROPHETIC QUOTES*

Here are three prophetic quotes that may also stand you in good stead:

1. Most people face the future with their eyes firmly fixed on the rear-view mirror. (*Marshall McLuhan*)

2. History always repeats itself: the first time as tragedy, the second time as farce. (*Karl Marx*)

3. How do I know it's right? No one's ever done it before. (*Nervous client of mine.*[9])

*SETTING ASIDE VISITING TIME*

Have faith in your talent-spotting abilities. When you've identified the authors of the best ads about, examine their territory. **If you've never encountered the agency whose work you admire, pay a visit to explore the environment and meet the people.**[10] Discover whether they have unlocked a new way, a fresh outlook. Chances are, you'll learn something of value.

## WHAT?

Having discounted hype, remember that some of the big names in the business have genuinely earned their fame. Many of these men and women are genuinely inspirational to all who work around them. But:

9  He was persuaded to run it. It picked up all sorts of decent awards and the brand, twenty-five years later, remains healthy.

10  Proposition No. 28.

◆ *BEWARE all the others. They reinforce the cynical view that, when egos are being measured, the known cosmos is uneasily small.*

◆ *BEWARE the big stars, because the more stellar their reputation, the more unlikely they will be to share the same room as your business.*

◆ *BEWARE the glamorous new business team. In the larger agencies, they are sleek bait in Comme de Garçons suits, present only to attract – but never to work on – your business. Like polished seducers, of course they'll love you for ever, although you may never see them again (until they write to you from their next agency offering you the earth).*

Chances are that, even if you're not clutching one in your hand, you'll probably be carrying a mental checklist. Generally, liberated clients seek:[11]

11  And if they're not, they should be.

1. independence of stance;
2. a fertile environment;
3. intelligence of solutions;
4. innovative approach; and
5. bold executions.

*BEWARE:*

◆ *Ads that all look alike;*
◆ *Ads that follow the same solution;*
◆ *Any mention of the term 'lifestyle';*

◆ *Any ads that look like anyone else's ads; and*

◆ *Ads that fail to move you.*

# LESSONS

### Proposition No. 24

*The agency must have a cracking reel.*

### Proposition No. 25

*The agency will never present more than one campaign at a time.*

### Proposition No. 26

*The agency has the guts to part company with clients on matters of
deep principle.*

### Proposition No. 27

*'When everyone is zigging, you need to zag'*
*David Abbott*

### Proposition No. 28

*If you've never encountered the agency whose work you admire, pay
a visit to explore the environment and meet the people.*

# STEP 8: THE CHOSEN PEOPLE

The ceremonial seldom changes. The priests gather around the boardroom altar and, like priests anywhere, exude an uncanny ability to make you feel slightly ill at ease. Decor and dress are designed to heighten that feeling of insecurity (the cynical among us could almost get the feeling that unscrupulous agencies exploit both to their short-term gain).

Sebastian Suit, your account director, rose at 5.30 am to select a sincere tie from his rack for all occasions. The sweaty creatives were also awake at 5.30 am, not having slept all night, busy in the studio preparing cardboard for the meeting. Sid Vicious, the creative director, has been rehearsing the scripts and polishing his best lines.

You've shaken hands, shared nervous jokes and one of the female leads from *Baywatch* has filled your coffee cup to the brim. Nervously, you've scribbled the date of the meeting on your personal pad with the monogrammed agency pencil. And you've surreptitiously snatched the discreet matchbox to leave mischievously at another agency meeting.

You've stirred your coffee. You've returned all the synthetic smiles around the table. And now the agency is about to reveal the creative proposals derived from your brief. As the uninitiated waiting to view the mysteries, you are about to enter uncharted terrain.

Every client presentation I've ever attended is possessed of its own range of dynamics, usually fuelled by anxiety, ambition and fear of failure. Two different cultures are confronting one another. Both are swearing allegiance to the same objectives and strategy, but both are nursing differing agendas. The client wants a campaign that sells the product, and the agency wants a campaign they can put on the reel. Sometimes, the two are not compatible.

Every advertising agency is an uneasy coalition, the degree of unease dependent on the age and ownership of the company. Once upon a time in Britain, agencies were a cross-section of all the social classes: officer class executives, *louche* middle-class intellectuals as writers, lower-middle-class artists as designers and downright working-class oiks as the production department.[1] Nowadays, the types are different – more professional and slightly more difficult to tell apart – but the major schism remains.

Basically, one guy is trying to run a business and another is trying to run an art gallery. If the two are talented and both talents coexist in harmony, then success often flows. But if there is a talent imbalance, discord is inevitable. The creatives (eternally paranoid) will always be distrustful, convinced that the management are selling their more radical ideas down the river to keep the financial director happy. Personality conflicts will develop. Politicking sets in. And, together with the already rampant paranoia, fine agencies can be reduced to husks. As Tony Blair once ruefully observed (before he became Prime Minister) **'In politics, you sometimes despair of having a sensible debate.'**[2]

1   True story, as witnessed by my ex-partner, Barry Bryant, on New Year's Day (1973, I think), before it had become a public holiday. Agency meeting scheduled for 9.00 am and staff gather in boardroom. 10.00 am, chairman turns up offering no apology.

'Terrible hangover from last night,' he barks. 'And the Bentley played up on the damn M4. Anyway, bad news. Clients have slashed billings. Profit forecasts are down, so there'll be no rises. Any questions before I go to lunch?'

Office manager raises his hand.

'Yes?' snaps chairman.

Office manager clears throat: *'Does that mean I can't get a new claw hammer?'*

2   **Proposition No. 29**.

## THE HIGH PRIEST

In any presentation of new advertising, the most awed silence is reserved for the creative director. He[3] is the High Priest, the most distinguished member of the priesthood, the key link between the raw creatives and you. When creative directors talk about creativity, there are no grey areas. Most subscribe to the prevalent Charles Saatchi school of advertising criticism: '*It's either brilliant or shit.*'

As High Priest, the creative director is the most important figure in any agency. While the other functionaries can write reports or choose sound burgundies at lunch, only he has the power to extract campaigns from the creative department. And it is his judgement that deems whether an idea or execution will be presented.

Occasionally, he is difficult to identify by costume. If the agency is offering a bland solution, he may deck himself out in avant-garde *schmutter*. If, however, the solution is radical and wacky,[4] the outfit will be the very model of fine gentleman's tailoring.[5]

It's one of those immutable laws: meetings and creative people are incompatible. Yet, in ad agencies, those harbingers of the future, those organizations gifted with second sight, those oracles with their forefingers on the pulse of the future, what happens all the time? There, languishing in some airless chamber filled with debating suits, you'll find a highly expensive, senior creative idly

[3] If you are pointing an accusatory finger at my un-PC-ness, I apologize. But I employ the masculine for creative directors in the knowledge that the majority is male. And the handful of women who have reached the post behave like toreadors.

[4] '*Radical & Wacky. Good morning, how can we help you ...*'.

[5] A route corroborated by Tom Peters, the US management guru, quoted in the *Independent* as saying: 'I was taught by a boss twenty years ago that if you are going to preach madness, better show up in a conservative suit.'

doodling on a scratch pad, desperately devising an excuse to exit and make some serious progress elsewhere.

Somehow, you'd have thought that management consultants would have impressed upon agency bosses the wisdom of cosseting their talent, like making more efficient use of resources by superglueing the noses of their prophets to the office crystal ball.

Efficient? *Ha*! Don't make me croak my hollow laugh. Anyone who has spent any time[6] as creative director of a large international agency is extremely aware that a hefty percentage of precious time is wasted faffing around in pointless meetings and inconclusive conferences. Many agencies display their creatives like trophies ('Look who we've got working on your business'). The motive ('Our creative management is *totally* involved') might be clear, but the reality is foggy.[7]

Incarcerated in boardrooms, the tedium would reach such peaks of intensity that I tried to master the esoteric skill of yawning through my ears. Because my contribution was seldom expected to climb above nil,[8] my efforts to appear attentive caused my coffee intake to rise as my boredom threshold lowered. And, compared with some of the meetings I have been forced to attend, ecclesiastical discourses about angels on pinheads would have been both fascinating and absorbing.

But this is not meant to be yet another polemic about committees.[9] The point of this mini-sermon is simple: **Your agency should provide you with substance, not pretence.**[10]

---

**6**    I have: 7½ years.

**7**    There was also a UK cider company that insisted its marketing executives made parachute jumps with the SAS.

**8**    The new US marketing director of a US confectionery company once insisted that all senior creative executives attend a Nielsen — at 8 am. I had never attended a Nielsen in my life and, at about 8.45, totally confused by the inexplicable charts, I thought it would be appropriate to ask an intelligent question.

'What's JJA mean?' I enquired.

'June, July, August', came the icy reply, accompanied by low-level account-handling sniggers. I stirred my coffee in silence.

**9**    Rather, it's a peg on which to hang Nietzsche's observation: (see page 200).

**10**    Proposition No. 30.

Anyway, as far as clients are concerned, creative directors should be sparingly applied. A strange lot, they're an unstable combination of ego and insecurity. They prefer not to know that, out there in the rest of the world, there might be people who can surpass them in wit and inventiveness.

If that sounds a little far-fetched, allow me to illustrate with a quote in a pre-Christmas 1996 issue of *Campaign* from Mark Wnek, high priest of Euro RSCG, who said: '*Every time I see a great ad done by someone else, a part of me dies.*'[11]

Universally, few jobs equal the creative director's because it also involves the management and constant recruitment of a creative department, a specialist role not for the faint-hearted. The rewards for success can be generous, but the wages of failure are disastrous.

A long-retired creative director once confided to me that the job was a cross between managing a Premiership football team and running an unruly kindergarten.[12] His description was dead accurate.

A creative director's main function is to extract brilliant work from his department, relevant and on time. It sounds like a doddle, but it isn't. Ideas seldom occur when you need them, and so creatives have to be pressured. Creative directors need to be skilled in persuasion, dissuasion, threatening behaviour and encouragement. Occasionally, matters get out of hand and creatives hold fast to ideas either unpresentable, or off-strategy, or both. They need to be damped down, and re-routed (if not by gentle coercion, then by threat).

11  A sentiment not too many kilometres from that of Ferrari's chief designer (and if that isn't high priest enough for you, I don't know what is), Aurelio Lampredi, who observed on first driving a Mini Minor: '*If it were not for the fact that it is so ugly, I would shoot myself.*'

12  My son Jonathan contributed a fresh (to me) description of the creative director's role: '*herding cats*'.

Throughout the exercise, passions run well above the recommended safety levels and it is not unknown for resignations and dismissals to fly about.

All to be expected: creative departments are fuelled by passion (and lots of other recreational substances).

But, whether or not you approve of the means of raising inspiration, we've all got to get ideas from somewhere. When I was still a practising creative director, I would be continually grilled at parties by people in more boring businesses: *'Aren't you scared you'll ever run out of ideas?'* (the line of questioning seldom altered). To which the answer was always a toss of the head and a fate-tempting, carefree laugh.[13] Advertising creatives don't have time to enjoy the luxury of being tormented by writer's block, but should their muse ever take an extended vacation, they could do a lot worse than follow the advice of Ron Collins, former distinguished art director and one of the founders of the agency WCRS, as quoted in *Campaign*:

13    The honest answer, of course, was *'bloody terrified'*.

> *Occupy yourself with anything but the problem (sex, drugs, or rock 'n' roll are recommended only in moderation). During this passive state, while the mind is free of tension, the solution will present itself as if by magic.*
>
> *Warning: the best results are achieved by those who keep their reservoirs topped up. Visiting art galleries, reading books, listening to music, even watching TV is more likely to trigger original thought processes than a flick through old award-winner annuals and style magazines.*

## THE BOOK

*Q:* What does Mr Collins mean by 'old award-winner annuals'?

*A:* He means 'The Book'.

*Comment:* Eventually, we had to arrive at the subject of the Holy Writ, 'The Book'.

To US creatives, it's the One-Show Annual. All over the world there are competitions that publish annuals and reviews. But to British creatives, there is only one 'Book', the annual of the Design & Art Directors' Association, sometimes erroneously called DADA, but actually D&AD. And British creatives devote considerable creative energy to getting their work accepted and published in their Book. Because, for creatives, The Book has overridden its earlier status as the Holy Writ to become the primary object of worship because work is only selected for The Book when it has been deemed suitable by a committee of High Priests. Once your work is in The Book, you have begun to ascend the Sacred Pyramid and a reasonable price has been attached to your head.

Creatives whose work is accepted for The Book on a regular basis are deemed worthy of being invested somewhere as High Priest. Therefore, to any ambitious young creative, nothing must bar the way to inclusion in the hallowed pages. Not a brief. Not a threatening creative director. Not even a livid client.

*DOWNSIDE ALLEY*

*Q:* Is The Book a catalogue of great marketing triumphs?

*A:* Yes. And no.

**Comment:** Of course, for it's packed with famous campaigns and startling pieces of advertising. But a few hours invested in leafing through old Books actually reveals that they serve as tombstones to multiple major marketing disasters. Indeed, while juries might have lauded many of the ads, punters in the market-place deemed the brand a turkey.

Moreover, many items never actually saw client approval or even light of day. It has been known for frauds to be selected. Never underestimate the ingenuity of creative people when trying to force entry into The Book.

While I would be first to admit that D&AD has been a considerable power for good and has been a positive influence in the high quality of British communications, I cannot overlook its negative effect upon creatives eager to make fat reputations and big bread.

Because, every year, the new edition of The Book (like couturiers) sets a style, it can exercise a pernicious influence on work for your brand. Immature creatives feel that, by following the Style Police Dictates, they will crack The Book (wrong, for every reason that you can imagine. Prizes are never awarded to copycats). Having your ads tailored for The Book rather than the market can lead to disaster.

It is absolutely vital, nevertheless, that you have the latest copy of The Book in your office. It tells you which agencies are in (and, by omission, tells you who are out). You need to know the state of creative play for bits of the consumer's mind, because that's your battlefield.

Do I need to italicize for emphasis? **You need to know The Book and its contents**.[14] And, if you think that an ad is being designed for The Book rather than your brand, my advice is to state your reference, stand your ground and turn it down.

14 Proposition No. 31.

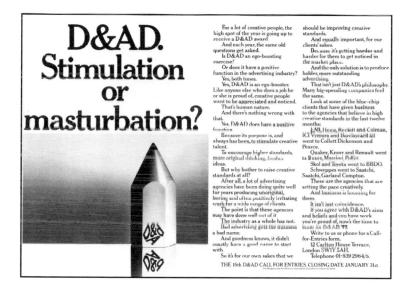

*A rare moment of honesty in advertising. The question hasn't departed (in the 70s, at least you could still pose the conundrum). Interesting navel-gazing item: this ad aimed at worshippers of The Book was voted into The Book*

Am I overstating my case? Not if you pay attention to *Campaign* journalist Stephano Hatfield, who commented:[15]

15    *Campaign*, 6 February 1998.

*… if you wanted an accurate record of the best British advertising over the past 20 years, you won't get it by looking at D&AD pencil winners. The level of personal prejudice and ganging up that used [?][16] to take place made the behind-the-scenes shenanigans at the average ice-skating championships look tame.*

16    Stephano's question mark, not mine.

I've been there, and he hasn't used a word of exaggeration.

17    *Campaign*, 15 May 1998.

And while chomping through my breakfast branflakes a few months later, I read *Campaign*'s report[17] of the previous night's D&AD awards. And any comments I have made about the creative Style Police were not only justified, but reinforced. Nothing changes. In the magazine's 'Close-Up' section, reporter Caroline Marshall wrote:

*A bigger issue, and one that Seymour will find even harder to address, is what Delaney calls the 'blocking' of awards and the yobbishness of an audience too mean-spirited to clap the work of peers… The big issue is the venality of the judging; there's still a coterie of people who get together to control the whole process.*

Mr Delaney is right. And Ms Marshall continues:

*The 'system' means that an unfashionable agency, such as Delaney Fletcher Bozell, stands little chance of winning the*

*award every agency, copywriter and art director covets most…
this elitism, peculiar to D&AD, where some jurors appear to
have decided that their subject is fine art, not commercial art,
is one of the things about D&AD that is a lot harder to
change…*

And later in the same issue, *Campaign*'s leading article adds thun-
derously:

*… the feeling was that D&AD judging is actually all about
mean-spiritedness.*

*It's a malaise* Campaign *encounters at our awards in the jaded,
cynical reaction to the winners. BTVA, Cannes and* Campaign
*have tried hard to stamp it out in their own judging. From the
evidence of our own eyes and the feedback from depressed jurors
at D&AD, it is still rife…*

Although it's difficult to keep sight of this in the midst of 2,500
creative people at Olympia,[18] this is not what the advertising
business is about.

18 The exhibition hall,
not the home of
Zeus in Greece.

## THE POLITICS OF CREATIVITY

*Q:* If creativity is so troublesome, why do agencies have creative
people at all? Indeed, what are creatives for?

*A:* Getting your ads noticed.

*Comment:* If an ad doesn't get itself noticed, all other considera-
tions are academic (85 per cent wastage, B Bernbach). Thus

**Proposition No. 32: An ad's first duty is to draw attention to itself.**

When the old tycoons were boasting about half their budget being wasted, they didn't know the half of it. Planning and research beaver away to try to locate your market; media hunts them out; and the role of creativity is to get noticed and squeeze the message into that elusive 15 per cent.

And there's the problem. Planning, research and media can be described as semi-scientific disciplines. Creativity, on the other hand, (regardless of the pseudo-scientific claims of Hopkins or Reeves) defies the description 'discipline'. Creative people are a breed apart: they're actually born that way. Who and what are they?

Perhaps you've never noticed, but there are at least four different kinds of creative person:

1.  *The unskilled and incoherent.* He got the job because he looked the part and survives for as long as his brute strength and raw aggression hold out. Because only then can the agency recruit enough volunteers to eject him from the building.

2.  *The skilled and incoherent.* He has no desire to be creative director; 'I just want to be in The Book.' If he manages constantly to recast his style to accommodate the vagaries of current fashion, he will be an asset to solid, unstartling agencies for years.[19]

**19**  One is reminded of Gore Vidal's comment (and barely concealed talons) on the subject of Andy Warhol: *'a genius with the IQ of a moron'.*

3. *The untalented and articulate.* Brilliantly glib at interviews, his ability to con gullible agency management about his talent (both creative and management) is famed in trade press exposure. And, while the agency bosses had half-heartedly believed the promises, they couldn't believe the product. Consequently, his total inability to deliver has seen him amass a fortune by being fired from a series of short-lived but generously paid jobs.

4. *The talented, skilled and articulate (TSA).* The cream. The Holy Grail. Every agency manager's quest. Very desirable, very popular quarry.

   *Comment:* if not careful, TSA develops a weight problem from too many meals bought by charming and attentive head-hunters. If able to avoid high-octane flattery, TSA will remain where the atmosphere is conducive to making good ads, eventually working up the company ladder to leadership.

Occasionally, TSA starts up a shop to pursue individual vision. But sometimes the TSA is tempted by large sums of money dangled by large bland agencies to become Creative Director, and 'turn the place around'. The TSA's rationalization for joining is: *If it doesn't work, it's their fault, not mine. If it succeeds, I did it all by myself.*[20] The argument never works; it's a fallacy. **An agency with a fading reputation can be turned around by nothing less than a cataclysm of cosmic proportions.**[21] Collision with a medium-sized comet, for instance.

20 Well, that and a sackful of money.

21 **Proposition No. 33**.

22    With recovery by
      no means
      guaranteed.

Unless part of a major surgical operation,[22] the TSA is nothing more than one of those tiny Band-Aids used to keep small children from grizzling too much. And our TSA is on a painful trip to nowhere. Having entered the agency on a massive ego boost, the TSA discovers that all advertising talent is diverted first into management and second into politicking.

Over time, any TSA with half-decent intelligence susses the agency's weaknesses and identifies them. Unfortunately, all the people, collectively or individually, own a substantial portion of the company, are crucial to a large piece of business, or are someone's lover or someone's ex-lover.

As a general rule, agencies shrink through an overdose of compromise. Too much compromise infects an agency. Fear blunts the skills of compromise. Responding to client criticism as an instruction rather than the beginning of a conversation exposes the agency to accusations of weakness. And at the first sign of weakness in an agency, *a client exits.*

Furthermore, surrender to clients sends a bad signal to the creative director and department. 'We don't have the confidence to sell your work whole-heartedly.' And when the agency is permanently in the wrong, *creative talent exits.*

TSA discovers agency employees are so dispirited, insecure and untalented that they are unable to produce exciting ideas. And, even if they were able, the agency couldn't give them away. But, presentation being all, TSA's been drafted into an international client confidence-building tour that involves weeks of either sitting in airline club lounges or meeting the client. '*Seems nice enough,*' the client representatives murmur cautiously. '*More understanding than the previous arrogant bugger.*'

Soon the rest of the agency board is echoing lines like: '*Best suit in the place,*' marking the end of TSA's domestic life and marriage. Instead of making ads or inspiring other people to make ads, TSA is dispatched to extinguish fires far away from home. But home is where the real fire is – caused by the smouldering discontent of an ignored family. At weekends, TSA is locked away in the study scribbling first thoughts (not always the best) and knowing that Monday morning, at 7.15 am, it's back on the Shuttle to another combat zone.

Nerves are unravelling. Creative energy, sapped by politicking, glides on autopilot, losing height. The combative spirit, consumed by stress, is heading nosewards very fast. And accelerating.

## You can't buy it

Creative talent cannot be acquired. Not for money. Not for love. And, being devoid of any discipline, it sets traps for management, as veteran adman Winston Fletcher observed:[23]

> ... A study at the Institute of Chicago School of Art, for example, which compared art students with the general student population, showed art students to be more introspective, socially aloof, self-sufficient, radical, experimental and non-conformist. The differences were not so vast, but they were significant – and have been broadly confirmed by other research.

23  *The Guardian*, 6 April 1998.

*And while it is true that all human beings are creative up to a point, it is also true that everyone can hit a ball over a net, up to a point. Very few have the talent to play at Wimbledon. (As in tennis, the creativity of uncreative people can only be improved very slightly by training.)*

Fletcher continues, quoting film producer David Puttnam:

*When you start out, you are describing something amorphous, which you are encouraging or asking them to create. This is a very specific management problem [involving] particular skills almost as rare as creativity itself.*

But that doesn't mean it is incapable of being assessed, judged or rated. You only have to know how. And, more importantly, *who*. Allow me to quote Ron Collins again, writing in *Campaign* in 1992:

*I've had the privilege of working with some of the most respected writers in the game and they were predominantly left-brained. Their thinking was logical, analytical and almost frighteningly computer-like at times.*

*On the other hand, art directors, being generally right-brained, work from gut reaction, synthesizing information at great speed, producing often-derided 'flashes of inspiration'.*

*That is not intended to demean art directors, but merely an explanation that their left brain does not provide the creative solution, it post-rationalizes it.*

*To a logical thinker who plans every step of the way to a solution, the idea of using intuition is not only anathema, it is positively frightening.*

How do creatives make a communication funny, interesting, or noticeable? The old journalistic advice works every time: **First simplify, then exaggerate**.[24] Pare the proposition to the bone to discover what emotion you're aiming for, and then consider how to approach it psychologically. When you've settled on the relevant stimulus, devise ways to dramatize it. In creative talk, it's called '*having an idea*'.

**24 Proposition No. 34.**

On the subject of simplifying, John Hegarty, iconic London adstar, writes:[25]

**25** *D&AD Newsletter,* March 1998.

*... if we are suffering from information overload, surely the answer isn't to overload our advertising. Surely the answer is to simplify. To make less say more. Not only does this view breathe added life into our work, challenging us to be more single-minded, daring and distinctive, but it also goes to the heart of creativity in advertising.*

*It is said that the foundation of wit is brevity. So it is with advertising. The power of our creativity lies in our ability to reduce, to simplify a seemingly complex brief down to a memorable, engaging idea. We are, or should be, skilled in the power of reduction. That is our art. We must, to succeed, recognize that we operate in the margins of the media. In the gaps in programmes.*

*We are creative guerrillas. We make our mark by arresting viewers' attention momentarily. And leaving them with a lasting impression. In a world that is suffering more and more information and clutter, the skill of our creativity conversely becomes ever more relevant. But only if we accept that reduction is part of our craft.*

Ideas are what make the stimulus digestible and memorable. You seek a suitable metaphor and then apply a treatment of shock, or horror, or showbiz glamour, or humour or fear. You can apply satire, parody or pastiche. Anything to get noticed.

Where do ideas come from? Ideas come from anywhere: topical events and recent stimuli such as movies, TV, videos, books, computer games and cartoons. Fragments, parallels, similarities, conjunctions, paradoxes and stolen items are filtered through personal obsessions, fixations, knowledge and experience.

The result is edited and shaped by the creator's own oblique approach to metaphor, language, music and visual image. And what emerges? An ad.

Of course, it is only a prototype ad, a rough. And, until it has been reviewed by the creative director, criticized by the rest of the management and approved by the client, it is not really a proper ad at all. *The client* – you, God's Chosen Representative On Earth, play either Breather of Life or Angel of Death. Because the ad can be:

◆ *sensationally brilliant;*

◆ *unsuitable;*

◆ *sensationally brilliant, but unsuitable;*

◆ *suitable, but awfully dull.*

The decision lies with you.

And you have to sleep with the decision.

Why is it simply not sensationally brilliant? Because very few agencies have true creativity.[26] Few agencies have the spark (and some that might have it wouldn't recognize it). There has always been a world shortage of talented people, explaining the most pressing problem in late twentieth-century advertising.

What I'm about to express seems to have slipped from the agenda at brand manager school and marketing director college. And yet it should be the first thing they instill into your brain. Dear Reader, take a deep breath.

# All creatives are not born equal.[27]

There, I said it. Elitist. But true. Twist the arm of any creative director who has spent a long evening interviewing keen applicants and the director will admit the truth: the world is full of wannabes, posers, writers and art directors with only half a good idea.

In reality, the creative world is inhabited by a very few giants and an awful lot of stunted pygmies. Fair's fair: how many great

**26** As previously mentioned, some agencies overcome their lack of talent by diminishing its importance and emphasizing their skills in the science of advertising. They invent ingenious formulas and clever ideas based on research, account handling or media skills in order to camouflage the fact that devising brilliant campaigns is pretty difficult, especially when you cannot attract decent creatives.

**27** Proposition No. 35.

composers, stand-up comics, Hollywood stars are there? Alive? And still you expect a non-stop run of brilliant, charismatic creatives.

Let us return to Bernbach: '*The real giants have always been poets, men who jumped from facts into the realm of imagination and ideas.*' And he added: '*An idea can turn from dust to magic depending on the talent that rubs against it.*'

'*Dust to magic.*' It even resonates with the authentic cadence of a Biblical prophet.

Now, after one shock to the system, are you ready for another? Here goes (and I realize it's hard to absorb):

28   All my Bernbach quotes from his speeches and articles, have been common currency in the business since I was a lad. Two books, *When Advertising Tried Harder* by Larry Dobrow (Friendly Press, US) and Bob Levenson's *Bill Bernbach's Book* (Villard Books, US), have been sources, but the most useful is a little book compiled by ad agency DDB Needham, entitled *Bill Bernbach Said?*

# All creative work is not born equal either.

If you've spent your working day hunched over boring printouts, it's not impossible that you could be seduced by miracles of presentation skills and glossy style. Bill Bernbach was alert to this possibility and warned creatives:[28]

*Merely to let your imagination run riot, to dream unrelated dreams, to indulge in graphic acrobatics and verbal gymnastics is NOT being creative. The creative person has harnessed his imagination. He has disciplined it so that every thought, every idea, every word he puts down, every line he draws, every light and shadow in the photograph he takes, makes more vivid, more believable, more persuasive the original theme or product advantage he has decided he must convey.*

*Furthermore, beware the fascination with technique. Used for its own sake, it can be disastrous. Because, after a while, you're so anxious to do things differently, and do them funnier and better and more brilliantly than the next guy, that that becomes the sole goal of the ad, instead of selling the merchandise.*

The rule is simple: adapt your technique to an idea, not an idea to techniques. Technique, like special effects in cinema, is best when invisible.

I have heard the argument that technique is useful to attract attention. Not if it's irrelevant, because the real skill lies in attracting attention *relevantly*.

Using the drawing below, a noted creative director used to lecture his department.

Readers will note this picture in an ad, he promised. And if it happens to be an ad for a device that stops money falling out of your pocket while standing on your head, it's a good device. However if it's an ad for something completely different, then the copywriter has to spend the entire first paragraph of the copy forging a link between the upside-down man and the product or service being sold.

Similarly, a picture of Pamela Anderson will attract attention, but simply becomes borrowed interest if she is simply being used to haul in the readers. Of course Bill Bernbach had a relevant comment about borrowing interest: '*You can get attention and really make people resent you if you do it with an unrelated gimmick. They won't like you for that.*'

## THE SADDEST TALE

As though everything else I've told you isn't dispiriting, here's some *really* dreadful news: even if we assume that the creative idea was OK, the cards are still stacked against you. If nobody notices the ad, it's dead, finished. Because, if it isn't in the élite category, namely those 15 per cent of ads that are noticed, everything – as the man pointed out – is academic.

Cruel but true: **The act of running an advertisement guarantees you nothing except expense.**[29] And the act of running an ad leaves you open to all sorts of abuses never contemplated. What law states that people must notice your ad? You must have watched readers turning over retailers' double-page spreads in broadsheets and tabloids. It's a big space, a tabloid spread, but

29   Proposition No.
       36.

perhaps the newspaper's editorial is more interesting that the dps. People do not buy newspapers to read ads.

Then again, remember this: stimulus and response are unequal. Asking someone to do something does not guarantee that it will be done. Or maybe the ad's look and tone are too bland. Or maybe while all the intentions were good, the execution was ham-fisted. It might have looked perfectly feasible on paper, but because of lack of imagination, or incompetence, or too little budget, or too many cooks, the result was a textbook example of reach outstripping grasp.

Perhaps we should rewind a tad to discover whether the problem started earlier. Perhaps the task was ill defined, for the wrong diagnosis of a problem can handicap any campaign. Perhaps the strategy was optimistic, pessimistic, ambitious or stupid. Perhaps all four.

Or perhaps the target was badly drawn, or the medium was badly chosen, or you were over-pushy, or didn't have a sufficiently good idea.

Or perhaps you hit vampire day....

## THE VAMPIRE PARABLE

Time for a long-overdue parable. There was once a brand of cognac called Salignac. And the Kirkwood Company's media department was jubilant at having applied considerable skill and negotiation to lock off the *solus* spot tucked into the highly influential *Londoner's Diary* in the London *Evening Standard*.

**30** Already assured of immortality as the louche talent who drew Wicked Willie, Gray is also the most shameless punster of our time. While lunching in a restaurant, a passing fan requested an instant pun. Without hesitation, Gray responded: *'Do you want a stale pun or a current pun?'* He also wrote the following headline for a Forte airport hotel: *'Out of the flying plane and into the foyer'*.

Grey Jolliffe,[30] the writer on the account, composed the strap line: '*Salignac, the old smoothie*' (well, the cognac had lain in barrels for three years and was very smooth, although an Irish whiskey is holding the current tenancy of the idea now). Next to a picture of the bottle, the headline schmoozed: '*Trust you to be where it's all happening, you old smoothie.*'

Well, *Londoner's Diary* is one thing, but the following page is another.

First week, there's the Salignac ad, and there across the margin is a photo of a poor US family clinging to a raft in devastating Mississippi floods. Second week, tornadoes and their path of damage through the US mid-West were opposite the ad. Third week, Colonel Amin's Ugandan death camps were illustrated with the first vivid pictures smuggled out of Kampala. It became known as the Curse of Salignac, and on Thursdays, agency staff stayed home, heads under duvets, when ads were about to run.

*That* vampire.

Back to Hades. Perhaps:

◆ *you weren't dramatic enough in your space, your time or your presentation; or*

◆ *you did all of those but you didn't upturn the convention sufficiently; or*

◆ *your ad was irrelevant to the readers or viewers; or*

◆ *it was a clone of someone else's ad but not as well done; or*

◆ *it was not very clear in its portrayal; or*

◆ *it was badly timed; or*

◆ *it was simply a really bad ad in a pathetic campaign.*

*YOU'RE FIRED*

Pathetic campaigns exist only because someone at the client's company wants them. If the client does not want them, the agency should have been persuaded to do something better. If the agency could not improve on its offering, the client ought to issue the order to fire.

But maybe the client cannot fire the agency because one of its most important directors is your chairman's cousin. Or it is the international system agency appointed out of head office. Or, worse, they might just be an appointment of the last few weeks (well, hard luck for being conned by such a bunch of second-hand car salesmen). In the case of all three, your hands are plaited behind your back unless you're a pretty tough cookie – in which case, you probably have a great future in marketing. Knowing your mind is good. Knowing when your mind should be expanded, and by whom, is even better.

## A LITTLE RAY OF SUNSHINE

Now that you're reduced to quivering jelly, I promise to start being positive again.

Advertising is a process. Every ad you're asked to approve is another step forward in that process. Or should be. If you feel it's a retrogressive step, say so.

Every ad should be an advancement of the brand's myth. In the light of that statement, take time off to study that myth. What emotions are you satisfying? What are your mystical powers? What miracles have you promised? Now look at what's on offer. If it doesn't reinforce the myth, scrap it. If the myth itself is not clear, start clarifying. Time is running out.

Use art. Art exists because ordinary life is exceptionally dull. Even the most sophisticated people pay to bring art into their lives. Use art to unsettle, seduce and amaze. Get the best artists to develop your imagery. The better the artist, the more indelible the imagery. And, once exposed, the images aren't forgotten.

Creative departments hunt endlessly for indelible imagery because they spread the message of a campaign far beyond the narrow confines of the paid-for media schedule. John Hegarty reminds us:[31]

> ... the greatness of an idea can be measured with the speed with which it enters our consciousness. The faster it does so, the longer it is likely to stay there. Remember the space you are buying is not on a poster site, TV commercial or in print. **It is inside someone's head. That's the only space worth buying.**[32] And it is in that space that I want my idea to open out, not on a piece of printed paper.

Throughout the ages, artists have proved their ability to touch the emotions and to presage the future. Which explains the patronage of the Authorities since before formal dating began.[33]

**31**   D&AD *Newsletter*, March 1998.

**32**   **Proposition No. 37**.

**33**   To keep them occupied so that they cannot cause trouble. And to have them working to the Establishment's own ends.

For instance, arts and craftspeople have always served religion. Some of the greatest creatives of all time – painters, sculptors, architects and musicians – have been on the church payroll, but when the church's funds were running low or the artists' faith began to falter, princes and nobles took over the chequebook. The power of princes (and their patronage) devolved to politicians, who have never been slow to use the art of persuasion to further their own ambitions.

But the power of the churches transferred to the new princes, who conduct businesses, control empires and manifest themselves as brands. These brands are worshipped by the masses who are grateful for the wonders they have wrought.

Meanwhile, nothing's changed for the artist, except the nature of the patron. Your having donned the prince's mantle, you still need the very best creatives working on your propaganda. To create means make, invent, conjure something absolutely new. And, as we have seen earlier in this chapter, only good creatives create. The competent merely embellish the ordinary.

Nothing (apart from your competitor's factory burning down) can benefit your brand so much as good creatives coming up with truly original ideas for you. The key word is 'original'. True creativity seldom needs to borrow; it touches on reality to release the imagination.

Ads really start working when execution and content are inseparably fused. And they work even better when your creatives are geniuses because, in the work of a genius, execution becomes content as well. Brilliant creatives don't give you what you want: they give you what you never knew existed. Take it from me, it's rare, but you'll know it when you see it.

## THREE HINTS

Want to build a client–creative relationship based on mutual respect? Then assimilate these three pieces of advice:

### 1. Keep the lid on manufactured panic

In August, the silly season drapes itself about the metropolis like a poultice. Outdoors, asphalt suppurates. Indoors, the whine of the air conditioning fails to silence the familiar nature calls of late summer: 'Make the logo bigger,' 'Why do we need so many people on the shoot?,' 'What *does* a grip do?,' 'Nobody reads long copy,' 'Have you used the best takes?,' 'That photograph is too dark,' 'Are you sure that was really forty seconds?,' 'Shouldn't the logo be on longer?,' '*How* much?!'

These are the calls of the Flapping Brand Manager, a species that should be sojourning on some blistering Mediterranean rock but is delayed in an ad agency conference room being forced to approve quotes/rough-cuts/proofs in time to make the Migrant Marketing Director's holiday departure unruffled.

'The Marketing Director is making his annual migration to the Seychelles on Friday and needs to be satisfied that everything is neat and tidy.' Although the thermometer is nudging 30°C, the words freeze the arteries of creative directors everywhere. (Nearly as chillingly doom-laden are: 'I know we're only on air at Christmas, but we have a September sales conference and I promised the salesforce...'.)

I have never seen an ad whose development was improved by panic. Nor have I seen a campaign whose launch was made better through haste. Haste and panic give birth to the cock-up, the dog's dinner and the haunting embarrassment. And, close by, eager to act as midwives, are petulant creatives, Neanderthal photographers, film directors with Battleship Potemkin-sized egos, account men whose grandmothers would appear to be interred at Lords, and typographers whose prime source of inspiration is the centre spread of *Exchange and Mart*.

Their songs are not unfamiliar. 'It's art, man.' 'Don't you want to get it in The Book?' 'Well, Heineken does it.' 'Of course you can reverse type out of four-colour half-tone.' 'Three-quarters of a million isn't a lot these days...'. 'Don't tell us it's dark *now*; you approved the Polaroids.' 'Look, fart-face, I was hired to shoot a fucking film, not point a camera at your crappy product.' 'It's the computer's fault.' 'I don't know why you're complaining now: you were at the shoot.'

And my personal favourite. *'The trouble with you is that you don't understand.'*

To my knowledge, there is no special training establishment for trainee Brand Managers. Outward Bound schemes for character building excite some manufacturing companies, but are less than useless because they ignore instruction on the appropriate size for a logo. Surviving off raw hedgehog spines for two days in a force-nine gale is more convivial than confrontation with a creative pair whose latest bid for gold you thwarted by turning down their script. Abseiling down 2,000 feet of ice-bound precipice, clad only in a jockstrap and armed with a Swiss army knife toothpick, might be admirable preparation for a successful career in the SAS, but it fails to prevent knees turning to aspic when confronted with a quote from a seriously fashionable production company.

I envisage an ivy-clad retreat where Brand Managers can attend lectures on visual awareness, musical appreciation (from plainsong to hip-hop), advanced film studies and a special degree in paediatric psychiatry. Plus parallel lessons in unarmed combat, skin-thickening, self-tranquillization through transcendental meditation and a special series on ego-nurturing. An ability to count from one to ten very slowly would be considered an advantage.

It would be a six-month residential course with irregular interruptions, no dislocating of work schedules for sudden sales conferences, and no unplanned departures of VIPs to vacation destinations devoid of fax, phone, carrier pigeon or cleft stick.

It might not equip Brand Managers to cut a bold swathe in Goose Green, but it certainly will teach them what a grip does.

*Moral*: Good campaigns are not born in haste.

## 2. AVOID FACTORY TOURS

Not twenty minutes after awarding the business, the client, bon-harmonious with house champagne, announces to the agency that 'It would be a good idea if the team came up for a factory tour.' A fortnight later, the ad agency team in hard hats, overalled and overawed, is standing by a thundering machine witnessing an arcane process which is being described by a man whose explanation is being drowned by the machine's thunder.

In Japan, they have refined this form of torture with great subtlety. The hard hat has a built-in set of radio headphones so that you can hear your guide's patter with little interruption, other than the incomprehensibility of his commentary.

Thinking terrible thoughts, I have cowered beneath the nozzle of a funnel containing 80 tons of strawberry mousse. In Japan, I have marvelled at uncomplaining robots fashioning a steel plate into a motor car with no visible human assistance. I have been thrown around test tracks and seen chickens trussed for the oven fired out of cannons and into jet engines. I have watched kettles, petrol pumps, computers, ambulances, cigars and sliced braised beef being assembled and packaged. I have watched wine being pressed and helicopter turbine blades being machined from titanium. The 70-per-cent-proof atmosphere leaving me reeling and legless at 10 am, I *think* I have watched cognac being distilled.

Horror-struck at a world-famous sauce factory, I watched our guide seize an anchovy (about the size of a medium-sized plaice, but much greener in hue) from a copper vat and swallow it whole.

(My chum Gray Jolliffe fared worse. When he was a copywriter on a pet food account, he offhandedly asked the brand manager whether the food was fit for human consumption. The eager young brand manager promptly dipped his hand into a *mélange* of assorted entrails, grabbed a dripping morsel and ate it. It was much, much later in the factory sick bay that Gray resumed consciousness.)

Why factory tours? Are clients insistent that the agency traipses around assembly lines and bottling plants when the embarrassed plodders understand little, remember less and learn nothing? Or do brown-nosing agencies use it as an opportunity for deep ingratiation?

Whichever is the case, Claude Hopkins should shoulder a hefty chunk of the responsibility. When the legendary copywriter observed during a brewery tour that all the returnable bottles underwent a compulsory steam bath, he tapped 'Our bottles are washed in live steam,' on returning to his typewriter, initiating a milestone in salesmanship and causing an advertising sensation. And, although only advertising archaeologists can remember the brand name of the beer, it served as the revelation for Rosser Reeves' book on the USP. Hopkins' immortal line  gatecrashed copywriting mythology and helped people like Robin ('*interrogate the product until it confesses its strengths*') Wight make a pile of loot. Personally, I have always wondered whether there is such a thing as *dead* steam.

The Hopkins School thrives. And through his legacy, creatives never cease to be deeply impressed by factory tours. Fascinated by the graphic antics of machines, they seek their own live steam stories and build them into ads, always (and quite correctly) rejected by the client on account of being too mundane and too damned dull. Unfortunately, it is an exercise the agency can neither evade nor avoid.

I cannot recall a single great campaign inspired by a factory tour.[34] The odd memorable ad about R&D, maybe. The deathless campaign, never.

The question remains: why are clients spring-loaded to suggest a trip to the mill? Allow me to ventilate six theories:

1. *As a form of agency initiation.* Here is where we make what you have to promote. We are showing you all our secrets so that you will know us, warts and all. This, incidentally, is a titanium sprodget. Very useful, sprodgets.

2. *A neurosis shared is a neurosis doubled.* We are partners now. Look at all these machines churning out product. Look at all those people working at the machines. If you can't sell it all, we will go broke.

3. *As boasting. We are pretty damn mega.* We are pretty damn rich. We are pretty damn unstoppable. The implication being that we are pretty nasty control freaks (will Winston Fletcher ever repeat the story about asking a question of an irate wristwatch client who became so incensed that he ordered Winston to walk around the warehouse to visualize the vastness of the task ahead?).

34  Alright, one. The marvellous Fiat commercial, showing building by robots. But that was Collett Dickenson Pearce at its very best. And somebody probably bet the team that they couldn't do a factory commercial.

4.  *Pride.* We may not be as stylish as you advertising chappies, but we create real things, not dreams.

5.  *Bonding.* We're all in this together and now you can see that the place where we work is not half as luxurious as the place where you work.

6.  *Embarrassment. Deep* embarrassment. Fly halfway across the world. Miss connection other end. Travel by high-speed train through night. Check in as other people are breakfasting. Shower. Come down to meet factory car. Head aching. Tour very big, very noisy factory. Retire to conference room. 16 mm projector switched on to explain with animated diagrams what we have just seen. Lights off. Comfy chairs. Lights come back on. Entire agency fast asleep. *Deep, deep embarrassment.*

Pride in the workshop is no fresh phenomenon. Once upon a time, clients insisted that the factory be illustrated on pack, letterhead and even in ads. Times might change; human nature does not. What is really important is product experience. Unless it is greener-than-thou, how it is made is pretty damn irrelevant, these days.

Arrange a factory trip by all means but do not expect it to hatch a campaign.

***Moral:*** When you and the agency stroll through the armature winding shop, the consumer can be left standing outside.

### 3. STAY AWAY FROM SHOOTS

Do you have a resident expert on film? Has anyone on your team ever studied on a film course? If you had, you'd know that studios and locations need to be avoided. And even though they sound like fun, you could land up crucified.

In the early video shoot days, the game of Confuse-a-Client was easy. An agency producer would place the client in a corner where, slowly, he or she would be silenced by the pitiless onslaught of visible technology. There is a limit to how many times a client can shriek 'What's *that?*' at a bank of monitors and be told (a) don't worry, we aren't recording, (b) it isn't on the screen in the centre, see? and (c) it's the camera operator's foot.

But it can be worse. Read what follows.

### WORST CASE SCENARIO

Happy with your new commercial? By now you have convinced yourself that you are. There was just that matter of the pre-production meeting. Where the director seemed to be less concerned with selling your product and more interested in shooting 'a sort of, kind of, like, German Expressionist monochrome thing'. He had flashed a lot of coffee-table books of terrifying women photographed by Hitler's girlfriend. He was radiating charisma and had three sensational blondes in tow. One of them was smoking a Turkish cigarette. A bit hazy now. Is your suspected ulcer playing up?

CUTTING UP ROUGH

Now they've presented the rough cut. It didn't exactly make you want to jump and punch the sky. Repeated viewings at your request didn't help a jot. The film appeared to depart from some of your most cherished storyboard frames. Particularly those where you thought you were going to spend long minutes with the camera caressing your pack. At least those were the creative director's words when he presented the script and storyboard.

And, although the creative team, and the editor, and the director, swore that the commercial was spot-on in length, it did seem to be less than the forty seconds. And you did not appreciate the way they sniggered when you asked if they had used the best takes, Even though it seemed a reasonable question at the time. After all, they shot so many things and so very few of them appeared to be in the commercial.

But how will the target market react? Or, more importantly, how will your irascible chief, *obergruppenfuhrer* marketing, react? His warnings about not letting the agency take wholesale advantage continue to career around the inside of your skull like a wall-of-death biker, while in the pit of your stomach something multi-pawed stirs.

And yet, and yet.

You were actually present on the set when every sequence was shot. *Or nearly everything.*

While they were shooting, you were in the production office, hunched over a mobile, almost melting with panic messages about being de-listed in Asda. Sophia, the delightful producer who seemed to be developing quite a thing about you, kept you entertained with hysterical tales of shoots that had gone massively awry. Punctuated by frequent meals, teas, snacks, pastries, coffees and beers.

EVERYTHING COVERED

They insisted they had covered everything. The director religiously showed you a small scribbled storyboard, all the while dealing with various technicians (*what do they all do?*). The lighting cameraman, who uses his Oscar statuettes as doorstops and who is Madonna's lighting cameraman by personal insistence, seemed slightly absent-minded when he ignored your plaintive suggestion to lose the shadow nudging the brand name on the pack. That was when the production company producer led you slowly, but firmly, away from the set. And Sophia came poutingly towards you, arms outstretched bearing telephone and currant bun.

BLACK LEATHER

The agency creatives seemed to be very occupied. They greeted you cursorily when you arrived and abandoned you to the account team. They appeared to be working hard, although most of the time they seemed to be laughing their heads off with the director. '*Bitchin'*,' they seemed to be saying, quite frequently.

Lunch was not bad at the local Italian. Lots of frascati and ravishing PAs in black leather. You must have been ever-so-slightly legless when you returned and had to wait uneasily outside the enormous doors while the red light was showing and could not enter the studio because they were 'turning over'. At least, that is what Sophia whispered into your ear.

Perhaps that was when they shot some of those odd sequences on the film. The blurred man with the over-pomaded hair. The flaming sugar cane field. The girl parachutists. You can't remember?

Frankly, you are losing bottle about showing the tape further up your company. Will they think you have blown it? Will you be accused of letting people run roughshod over you?

On the other hand, you may be fretting needlessly. They may love it. You may become a hero of the avant-garde.

*Be brave.*

## Beware

If you do go, remember you're with a film crew, who survive their hard life by living in a humour warp.

Agency I knew was filming a commercial in the Bahamas. Client, keen amateur man, takes camera to record location frolics and high jinks to show his wife, who is also keen on cine and travel. Also keen on snorkelling. And this is what he tells attentive film crew on flight to the island.

During break in filming, client's snorkel is spotted circling other end of lagoon and camera team gets to work. Opening a throbbing lowlife porn magazine purchased at Miami Airport, they do a brilliant job of filming a few choice pages with client's camera before putting it carefully back into its leather case.

It must have caused some consternation at the showing back home when they watched the cutaway from the palm trees at sunset. But nobody ever heard another word.

*Moral:* Plead a former engagement. Stay away.

Enough fun and games. Now *revise*.

# REVISE TILL IT HURTS

### Proposition No. 29

*'In politics, you sometimes despair of having a sensible debate'*
*Tony Blair*

### Proposition No. 30

*Your agency should provide you with substance, not pretence.*

**Proposition No. 31**

*You need to know The Book and its contents.*

**Proposition No. 32**

*An ad's first duty is to draw attention to itself.*

**Proposition No. 33**

*An agency with a fading reputation can be turned around by nothing less than a cataclysm of cosmic proportions.*

**Proposition No. 34**

*First simplify, then exaggerate.*

**Proposition No. 35**

*All creatives are not born equal.*

**Proposition No. 36**

*The act of running an advertisement guarantees you nothing except expense.*

**Proposition No. 37**

*The only space worth buying is inside someone's head. (J Hegarty)*

# STEP 9: THE DAY OF JUDGEMENT

Choosing his words with care, the High Priest starts his sermon and, slowly and deliberately, exposes the sins you've committed on behalf of your brand. You are scourged for buying and running the last campaign. You are pilloried for having been less than generous with the sacrifice. You are lashed for not possessing sufficient faith.

But the ritual excoriation is only a prelude to a miracle. Because the High Priest is about to unveil fresh iconography: your new campaign. Hark as he sings its praises. This new campaign will cleanse your brand of all impurities and rid it of the unholy accretions gathered from adhering to other dogmata.

The miracle will only work if you believe. If you maintain faith. You try and remember the articles of faith as he reveals the first of the tablets. The rhetoric may be (as the posh car dealers put it) pre-owned.[1] There's a 10–1 chance that he may use the mystical formula: '*We need to take the target by the scruff of its neck and shake it out of its slough of apathy.*' And what he means is, he is about to apply shock treatment. Oh dear: *shock.*

## FIRE!

Many creatives, particularly when young, attempt to camouflage lack of experience with an excess of attitude. An innate romantic instinct prompts them to imagine themselves as rebellious anarchists whose prime aim is to inflame the bourgeoisie, destabilize

[1] I promise I once saw a sign outside a Los Angeles antique shop, which said: '*All our merchandise is guaranteed age-enhanced*'.

the status quo and invite apocalypse. They employ the verbal equivalent of the head-butt,[2] because, to them, success is measured in how quickly (a) they can stimulate reactions ranging from disgust to anger, and (b) they can awaken the sleepy watchdog at the Advertising Standards Authority.[3]

Now this is not to deny that shock headlines cannot add a touch of drama and can even attract attention. But travellers down that route ought to remember that they become subject to the rule that states that there is a finite limit to how many times you can shout the word '*fire*' in a crowded auditorium and not be silenced by violence.

As a vehicle for expressing ideas, bad manners has a limited shelf life,[4] recalling Oscar Wilde's observation about the journalist and adventurer Frank Harris: '*Frank has been invited to all the best homes in England. Once.*'

But can shock pay? Naturally, there is a major exception to prove the rule: only one advertiser has made shock a stock-in-trade[5] and maintained the invention consistently and the pressure successfully. No surprises: of course I mean Benetton.[6]

Benetton's startling, often disturbing, poster campaign has fallen foul of both moral guardians and advertising politics. Personally, I find it curious, yet instructive and amusing, that the creative style police, in their rigidity, are discomfited by ads that achieve massive noting well beyond their adspend.

**2**    Colloquially known as '*The Glasgow Kiss*'.

**3**    Watchwords: 'legal, decent, truthful, honest'. British consumers don't need to be reminded about '*FCUK advertising*' for French Connection.

**4**    At the time of writing (late 1998), laddishness and bad manners get good audiences: *Men Behaving Badly* is a top TV sitcom, although moving the editor of *Loaded* to the more up-market *GQ* appears to have been a misjudgement.

**5**    Or should that be '*shock-in-trade*'?

**6**    Incidentally, Benetton is one of the very few advertisers that understand how to run a campaign *internationally*.

Paradoxically, the creative style police credo has always held that:

1. *ads should be confrontational;*
2. *all images must be as powerful as possible;*
3. *you shouldn't have to apologize or explain;*
4. *there's no need to show the product;*
5. *subject matter should be as controversial as possible; and*
6. *once is no evidence of skill — you've got to be able to come back for encore after encore.*

On the points listed above, Benetton scores very positively. So what explanation can be delivered for the verbal mauling and public barracking of Benetton's creative director by a cadre of style police officers when he addressed a D&AD seminar in

London? Mischievous thoughts: (a) not invented here, (b) he's a foreigner, and (c) the client does the ads himself.

If none of those, then we have to ascribe the reaction to sheer jealousy.

## HELP!

You know, in this world, there are people who twitch a little more than others. A moment's research into our backgrounds would reveal a shared experience: we have all performed international advertising award jury service.[7]

Have you ever visited Cannes in late June? The Côte d'Azur sun warms the *croisette*, the palm trees rustle their fronds in the light breeze, the girls are topless and you can actually feel the prices inflating all around you.

Cannes in late June means one thing to adfolk: the International Advertising Film Festival, where I have served as a member of the international jury (requiring 18 advertising people to sit in a darkened theatre watching commercials continuously for nine hours, every day for six days). The constant 30-second bursts of selling constitute such an awful exercise in sensory deprivation that, once or twice, I was tempted to report our predicament to Amnesty International.

Anyone who has survived the experience is unable to concentrate for many subsequent days on simple routines such as fastening a button, reading the time or ordering a glass of *rosé*

7    In this author's case: a past-presidentship of the London TV Awards, plus numerous juries over the years: Cannes, 1982; Ireland, twice; President of London Creative Circle for three years; D&AD, three times; Cleos, three times; and so on and so on.

without experiencing recall of some filmic image or other. But while advertising viewed *en masse*[8] for a week has a serious effect upon the psyche, it can be extremely instructive for those who live by it.

    Sadly, all ex-jurors will vouch that:

1. *Fresh solutions to old problems are extremely rare.*

2. *Most jokes are not funny.*

3. *Most enthusiastic housewives in commercials look like enthusiastic actresses trying to look like enthusiastic housewives and fail to convince.*

4. *Lots of people singing about the product is not an idea.*

5. *Mime is not funny, not convincing, nor an idea.*

6. *'Lifestyle' advertising is the rule.*

7. *Recent fads turn into hackneyed clichés: for example, if skateboards are the current fad, xty per cent of commercials feature skateboards.*[9]

8. *The Caveman lives – and seems to prosper.*

Nearly every juror has entered the screening chamber determined to give prizes to fresh treatments, cunning solutions and brilliant executions. And yet we were all amazed to see reel upon reel of current fad or fashion, and traditional aspirational formulas applied to all the old problems.

    Bearing in mind that entry to awards competitions is neither free nor cheap, why were the submissions entered in the first place? For a number of reasons, most of them out of control.

**8** In our case, some 3,500. Then reviewed as a short list of about 1,750, before being reviewed yet again for awards.

**9** Every year has its recurrent themes. Ours were nuns and chickens. Not necessarily together, though. Oh, and lovers in the rain. Every time another cliché would assert itself, a heartfelt groan rumbled through the jury. It would have been very instructive for the creators of the commercials to have been present.

The poor creative director has been playing King Solomon to every creative team in the department who wants work submitted. If the creative director tactfully suggests that 'Er, um, perhaps the entry is unlikely to get the jury leaping to its feet and punching the air,' the frustrated rejectee registers petulance that makes Adolf Hitler chomping the Axminster look like a dental hygienist demonstrating a new method of flossing.

The fees are indeed steep but, alas, we operate in a market economy. The demand is so prevalent and so powerful that, if the frustrated creatives can't persuade their agency to foot the bill for entering their ads, they *actually fork out the entry loot themselves.*

By severely pruning entries, the agency is not pinching pennies but reducing a crippling liability. Agencies do not have to be massive to dole out a sum roughly equal to Mrs Imelda Marcos's footwear budget in annual competition entry fees. The money is usually wrenched, stamping and shouting, from the New Business kitty. Maybe it should be reclassified under *Insurance*.

The reason agencies enter festivals in the hope of winning is that they figure awards impress new business prospects, reassure existing clients, and placate creative departments. And, of course, when one wins an award, the creative director's secretary is dispatched to the framers, certificate clutched tightly in her hand.

Clusters of framed certificates (the trendier the agency, the more *louche* their place of display – the gentlemen's toilet is not an unknown location) are a client's measure of judging whether or not an agency is 'creative' (the inverted commas are intentional. Really, the word should be 'fashionable').

By and large, agencies with walls full of the right certificates[10] fare better than agencies with few. Agencies with plenty of the right paper attract the hotter new business prospects and the creamier stratum of talent, but spare their weirdest effect for the agency's current clients.

While current clients adopt the affectation of knocking the idea of giving prizes to ads as irrelevant and absurd (at best), or mischievous (at worst), they manage to smile broadly when they hear that the industry has just garlanded one of their ads with a gong.

## A LITTLE APPRECIATION IS IN ORDER

You don't have to be Herr Doktor Professor Sigmund Freud to untangle the apparent contradiction. It is one thing for a client to take a chancy decision or act on faith. It is quite another to hear that it has been recognized and admired. But the best is knowing that your judgement has been vindicated and your act of faith rewarded and applauded. *In public.*

For what it's worth, here's my personal theory about agencies and awards. And it's elementary, really. Most agencies are so thrilled to have a film finally approved and signed off by the client, that its very existence becomes miraculous. It becomes like a child whose parents half-shut their eyes to its shortcomings. That it lacks charm, wit, entertainment, production values or subtlety is unimportant. The agency feels deserving of a prize simply to celebrate its existence.[11]

10  Most favoured: D&AD. Most established London competitions, *OK.* Almost everything else from abroad or international, *pffft.*

11  We all know the feeling. We simply don't enter it for competitions.

Put it this way, when you're a juror forced to view and categorize this unending stream of garbage, there has to be a logical explanation for the state of affairs. How it is that ad agencies, who claim to be arbiters of taste and discretion, hope to have their commercials declared winners when they should be declared dangerous industrial waste?

I am not alone in my condemnation. All jurors unite in marvelling that people have paid vast sums to enter unsuitable films. Current theory circulating among jury members sheds light on the lack of judgement shown by the agency creatives involved and the prevalence of industry ivory towers. It goes like this: there you are, working away at trying to solve your problem, oblivious of the fact that hundreds of brands/clients/agencies are simultaneously scratching their heads over the identical puzzle. And the solution is identical too: a synchronized application of current fashion, as seen by the film-maker at that moment.

12   Proposition No.
38.

To be blunt, **fashion is not an idea**.[12] And nor is a fad. There is probably nothing more old-fashioned than being up to date. It may be potent and record-breaking at the time, but where today would you find a brand that bolted itself on to the hula-hoop? Or the Beatles? Or the sun-dried tomato? Fashion is only window-dressing, unless it is the subject of the advertisement itself.[13]

13   In 1940, poetess
Gertrude ('a rose is
a rose is a rose')
Stein said: 'Fashion is
the real thing in
abstraction. The one
thing that has no
practical side to it.'

And that's where we find a curious phenomenon occurring: in the fashion business itself, copy (which used to be of the pizazz, let's-conjure-excitement-on-the-page variety) has totally vanished, leaving an example of merchandise and a carefully positioned logo to constitute the entire ad. This is able to cause consternation among the more dogmatic style police: 'Where's the idea?' they ask. Simple answer: the idea resides in the garment alone.

What perturbs the style police is that the idea in the product itself does not come from an agency creative team but from the named designer. The designer makes a statement and the statement endorses the brand. It needs no decoration by a wannabe when a genuine superstar designer can supply all the decoration by him or herself. Description is rendered superfluous and argument is irrelevant. The only copy is the address.

*Look Ma, no copy*

Cynics, however, with a dismissive sniff, will define all of *haute couture* as an elaborate PR exercise for the fragrance business.

## CUT ON THE BIAS

As handy links go, that wasn't bad. Because, if you don't mind, I'd like to stay with fashion for a moment, a helpful analogy when we discuss style.

Bear this in mind as you judge your next advertisement: writers, art directors, designers and film-makers of quality come in two sorts: extrovert and introvert. Neither is better than the other, and they coexist side by side, eternally like the North and South Poles.

At any stage in the history of visual design, two major schools coexist and their styles dictate fashion and polarize contemporary taste. One is the Roundhead style, the other is the Cavalier. Up-to-date equivalents, I suggest, are Armani and Versace.

On the positive side, the Armani school is minimalist, muted and understated. On the positive side, Versace is opulent, flamboyant and heavily ornamented.[14] The reverse also holds true, of course. Versace people would view Armani as dull, lifeless, inhibited and repressed. The Armani cult would see Versace style as loud, brash, vulgar, tasteless and over-emotional.

Two schools of thought, both in vogue at the same time. Meaning you have a dull post-modernist ad or a vulgar one. *Post-modernism.* The style we're about to depart from quite soon.

14   In religious terms, simply compare Lutheran and Russian Orthodox churches.

*Damn,* now we've raised post-modernism, we'd better deal with it. Please rewind to the Bernbach/Ogilvy Reformation. If we calibrate that as '*birth*' on the life cycle, then the subsequent development is '*growth*', bringing us to '*maturity*' sometime in the seventies (which, coincidentally, was the period when the advertising business, certainly in the UK, produced its choicest and clearest work).

So where are we now? We're at '*decay*'. Mannerism. A *mélange* of styles. Gratuitous ornamentation, knowing references and in-jokes, all lumped together under a catch-all description: '*post-modernism*'. The style ranges from Damien Hirst's pickled sheep, Tracy Emin's '*Everyone I have ever slept with*' tent, to Golden Wonder's Pot Noodle commercials.

This is not criticism, it is description: in a state of decay, all past standards are outdated, uncool, unhip. Past generation's disciplines may only be approached ironically. The visual appearance is often distressed, disfigured and distorted. In a wild display of glitz, Versace-ites will deliver a feast of rococo references, not necessarily unconnected. With a maximum of cool, Armani disciples will produce enigmatic work, minimalism pared to the point of invisibility, where only initiates are expected to guess an answer.

In decay, the profusion of styles leads to confusion of styles. In the search for visual newness, we see experiments involving every style of the past decades. When style itself becomes the ultimate issue, then content always loses. And when style is changing daily, watch out for those brands that base their communications on *lifestyle* advertising.

*Beware.* If you're relying on fashion and style to haul your brand up to date, you may find your communications majoring on a current sense of modishness, however odd, however unsuitable, and however irrelevant. And by the time you've shot your commercial, the fashion will be old hat. Nothing is permanent.

So, in order to avoid future confusion, I've included Laver's permanent chart of what's in and out. The very distinguished James Laver was Keeper of Costumes at London's Victoria & Albert Museum, and an incisive observer of trends. It's an invaluable guide to everything.

## JAMES LAVER'S FASHION CHART

| | |
|---|---|
| *Indecent* | 10 years before its time |
| *Shameless* | 5 years before its time |
| *Daring* | 1 year before its time |
| *Smart* | now |
| *Dowdy* | 1 year after its time |
| *Hideous* | 10 years after its time |
| *Ridiculous* | 20 years after its time |
| *Amusing* | 30 years after its time |
| *Quaint* | 50 years after its time |
| *Charming* | 70 years after its time |
| *Romantic* | 100 years after its time |
| *Beautiful* | 150 years after its time |

… and on to the classic.

Would you like to learn the difference between right and wrong in matters of style? Difficult. Ads work according to their own lights and in their own time. What one generation deems unacceptable may make a great campaign in a later generation.

## GOOD ADS

However, there are eternal practices that lead you towards a better ad. For instance, good advertising is:

◆ *centred around a single thought;*
◆ *rooted in simplicity;*
◆ *uncomplicated; and*
◆ *reduced to its essence.*

**Proposition No. 39: If we're in the reminder business, keep it simple.** Truly memorable slogans include the brand name and a proposition (*'Bovril stops that sinking feeling', 'Heineken refreshes the parts other beers do not reach', 'Guinness is good for you', BMW, the ultimate driving machine', 'Kellogg's Cornflakes, the sunshine breakfast', 'Beanz Meanz Heinz'*).

**Proposition No. 40:** (and the advice given by my favourite 20th-century artist, tenor saxophonist Lester Young, who always advised younger jazz musicians embarking on a solo) '**Tell a story, man.**'

Storytelling is the oldest communications medium on earth. Religions have thrived on parables. People love stories. People understand messages told to them in the form of stories. But stories need a theme, a form and, sometimes, even a moral. They also require a beginning, a middle and an end.

Levi's' best commercials tell stories. Any of the classic Bernbach output of the sixties tell a story: Avis is a company seriously dedicated to helping their customers; the Volkswagen is not only small but imbued with logic; Chivas Regal is a Scotch whisky with a remarkable taste; and so on and so on. Think how successful the Nescafé soap opera became, with media fame far in excess of the budget.

The trouble with getting good stories is that creative people of any quality carry an enormous amount of baggage in their minds. They have to sort it in the light of their obsessions and their subjective experiences. So allow time for a process of filtering and discarding because, once the creatives have jettisoned the junk in the attic, they'll uncover something fresh.

It might take more time. It might even jeopardize the date of the sales conference. But if it's good, it's worth it.

## SEEKING GOODNESS

If you are looking for more criteria, here are a few useful observations to kick around:

1.   *Good advertising is in tune with its target audience* – in terms of vocabulary: words, music, tone and visual style. Don't be patronizing; don't be distant. Make sure you're on the same wavelength. But bear in mind that sophistication and irony,

ill-used, can close the show by Thursday.

2. *Good advertising is challenging.* You stand a better chance of remembering a message that encourages you to think. Good ads engage the mind.

3. *Good advertising is cumulative in effect.* If nagging works, clever nagging works better, VW being the supreme example.

4. *Good advertising raises awareness positively.* Unless it's something you don't want people to do (like driving drunkenly or setting one another's dustbins on fire), the job of raising awareness must be allied to positive action.

    When I came into the business in London, there was a lot of chat about a cigarette called '*Strand*'. The ads had featured a Sinatra-type character, complete with hat and mac slung over shoulder, walking along London's Embankment alone and lighting a Strand. Everyone knew the ad. Everyone could remember the ad. The only problem was that no one bothered to buy the cigarette. They read it as the brand for people with no friends.

    Beware: raising awareness can also be easily achieved with a shocking display of bad manners. But beware: raising awareness negatively can be counter-productive. And any technique that doesn't benefit your brand must be suspect.

5. *Good advertising stimulates.* If an ad's first job is to get itself noticed, its second is to stimulate action. Performing neither is a waste of money. However, shrouded with '*but, but, but*', there's a massive warning lurking here:

# stimulus does not equal response.[15]

I once worked for a large car manufacturer whose marketing director used to bellow: '*Don't give me all this fancy advertising stuff. Why don't you just say: "There's never been a better time to get down to your local xyz dealer and buy one of our new models",*' almost as though consumers owed him one. Instructing people to do something does not guarantee that it will be done.

Human nature being pretty contrary, most people prefer to obey their instincts rather than some bossy individual.

Perhaps this explains the persistence of penal systems and the Ten Commandments (or, as Moses said: '*I've got good news and bad news. The good news is that I've negotiated Him down to ten. The bad is that He just refuses to shift on adultery.*').

*LET ME PAY TRIBUTE TO BOB MARCHANT*

Once upon a time, there was an agency called Papert Koenig Lois,[16] formed by the three eponymous guys who had broken away from Doyle Dane Bernbach. They were convinced by a British client that it would be a good idea to open a London shop, so they became the very first of the new wave of revolutionary US agencies to open in London. *Hot?* You betcha.

Peter Mayle[17] became their creative director and hired me as a copywriter, teaming me with an art director named Bob Marchant. A copywriter/art director team is like a marriage: the two halves work together, sharing each other's mind, to create something – campaigns.

Bob is Australian, tall, taciturn and deeply gifted. And we were able to produce such startling work that, about 18 months later, we found ourselves starting an agency called Aalders Marchant Weinreich.[18] One of our first gains was the surgical removal of the Burroughs Computer account from J Walter Thomson, then the largest agency in the world (we were probably the smallest).

It was at a Burroughs meeting that Bob showed his mettle. Peter Carney, our client, was a man facing the onrushing deadline for his annual report with the expression of a concerned blood-

16  Julian Koenig gained immortality as the man who wrote the classic 'Think Small', one of the very first VW ads.

17  Yep, the same one who made Provençal holidays famous.

18  When I sent a letter to my mother, who lived in Jerusalem, written on the firm's headed stationery, she replied '*Why is your name last?*'

*And how many did you break today?*

hound. 'What's the problem?' asked Bob. Peter let slip that the only thing standing between himself and disembowelment was a portrait photograph of his corporation president in Detroit, Michigan. 'Why?' asked Bob.

'Not even his wife can convince him to go out and pose,' said Peter, dark clouds gathering around him.

'No problem,' said Bob.

'What do you mean, "*no problem*"?' the client almost sobbed.

'You've got his home number?' asked Bob. The client nodded. 'Then ring his wife and tell her you've got a photo session booked with Lord Snowdon.'

'Bob, you're a genius,' said the client.

Of course, it worked. And the client was right: Bob *is* a genius,[19] with an intuitive grasp of the stimulus/response mechanism that deserves a Duke of Wellington Award.[20] Devising the appropriate stimulus to achieve the desired response requires precisely Bob's brand of genius, laced through with subtlety, diplomacy, tact and cunning (remember Br'er Rabbit and the Tarpatch?).

Unconventional stimuli can elicit very interesting responses two examples follow:

**19** Lost, alas, to the world of advertising. Having returned to Oz in the early eighties, he is now one of their foremost painters, with every exhibition a sell-out.

**20** If one does not exist, now is the time to invent it. Why Duke of Wellington? Picture the Great Exhibition, London, 1851. DoW is showing Queen Victoria around. She wonders whether anything can be done about the sparrow invasion.

The Duke doesn't miss a beat: 'Sparrow hawks, ma'am.'

◆ *When Pentax cameras, competing with Nikon in the seventies, had an image problem regarding the reliability of the brand, my creative team scored a hit with a Pentax campaign showing battered cameras belonging to famous people like David Bailey, Spike Milligan and David Hockney.*

◆ *At Wasey's, art director Steve Grime designed a Central Office of Information ad showing a car in the gloom with its headlights ablaze. Copywriter James Lowther wrote: 'To make this car disappear, put your fingers over its headlights,' a masterpiece of Rewarded Comprehension.*

# TO MAKE THIS CAR DISAPPEAR, PUT YOUR FINGERS OVER ITS HEADLIGHTS.

Block out the headlights above, and you'll get a good idea of how other drivers see you if you don't use your headlights on gloomy days.

The fact is they can hardly see you at all. And if you can't be seen, somebody can very easily get hurt.

This is one reason the law says you <u>must</u> put on your headlights when the daylight's poor. You can be fined up to £100 if you don't turn them on in conditions of daytime fog, falling snow, heavy rain or general bad light.

So remember the law. Remember the finger test. And be the bright one.

On gloomy days, put on your headlights.

See and <u>be seen.</u>

## IN POOR DAYLIGHT, BE SEEN. YOU MUST USE HEADLIGHTS.

Issued by the Department of the Environment, the Scottish Development Department and the Welsh Office.

Of course, one requires a receptive client:

A US cigar client once asked me to show him Collett Dickenson Pearce's exemplary Hamlet cigar campaign that 'I've heard so much about'.

When we'd passed the sixth commercial, he waved his cigar at the screen, saying, '*Enough. This has gotta be a brand for losers.*' Point neatly missed.[21]

The bottom line on good advertising is that it is ultimately *cost-effective.* Sensible, well-planned investments pay off. Once you've got a good campaign going, it's easier to invent vivid work in the same way as it is easier to develop funny or sad situations in a long-running sitcom.

The best examples in British advertising history are Hamlet cigars, Oxo stock cubes and Heineken lager.

## BAD ADS

The time has come to turn to Sin, and we should list a few sinful practices. For instance, where do the roots of bad advertising lie? Here are three suggestions:

◆ *in invention by committee;*
◆ *in design for the international division; and*
◆ *in the employment of a trendy commercials director.*

**21** It's about reverse miracles: when things are bad, they only get worse, so lighten up: Happiness is a cigar called Hamlet. The tradition of laughing-at set-backs can be traced through Norman Wisdom, and the US comic-book anti-hero, Sad Sack, to Charlie Chaplin and beyond, into Eastern European *shmendricks* (Yiddish: the guy unable to get it together).

*Comment:* trendy directors can be the cause of much aggravation. It's not that the script demands the trendy director's treatment; the real beneficiary is the creative team's reel.

The thinking runs thus: if he got three films into The Book this year, that's the way to get on. The agency doesn't argue, because his presence would benefit the agency reel as well. Faced with the agency's enthusiasm for the trendy director, the client politely acquiesces.

Disaster looms. Trendy director got that way by imposing personal will and trampling over agency and client wishes. To quote the famous theatre, film and TV director, Peter Hall:

> *No director is a god. If he's a god, or a tyrant, or an autocrat, or a master, then he is actually stopping the creative process happening, because he limits where things may go.*[22]

**22** The *Independent*, 11 January 1997.

And here are a few more suggestions to rid the world of inefficient advertising. Please don't imagine you've got a great campaign just because you've also got:

◆ *A trendy actor as the voice-over.* Every creative team wants to meet its idols for lunch, and the quickest way is to meet in the voice-over dubbing studio. Ask for something different and ruin the creative team's social life.

◆ *An adaptation of a well-known pop song.* If it's famous in its own right, why should anyone associate it with you?

◆ *Nostalgia as a vehicle.* If patriotism is the last refuge of a scoundrel, nostalgia is the second last. It's like saying, 'Please think of our packaged foods as bucolic and unprocessed because we call them *"Farmer Giles's Country Choice"*, even though they're vacuum-formed in a shed near Slough.' Broadcasting from a past where 'things were better' doesn't necessarily make a brand any better. And, anyway, it's only another tribute to Hovis.

◆ *The height of current fashion* (here today, gone…).

◆ *Ditto, next year's fashion* (too far out).

◆ *Or, ditto, last year's fashion* (ludicrous has-beens).

◆ *Special effects.* Either they are crucial to the storyline or they aren't. Anyway, they work best when they're invisible.

◆ *Flashy new video techniques.* They are a technique, not an idea. And don't let anyone tell you different.

◆ *A lavish budget.* Spending huge amounts of money guarantees nothing (consider the entire history of Hollywood).

◆ *Trying to shoot an epic on a shoestring.* Quite frankly, national TV is not the place to look tatty and naff.

◆ *Deviousness or even blatant dishonesty.* Not to be considered. You don't even have to set out with the intention of trying to con the punters. There are some of us around who remember the Air Canada campaign that asserted the cabin service was so good that nobody wanted to get off the aircraft. One long party, they hinted broadly. It was all intentional. And yet anybody who has ever flown will vouch that the moment the seat-belt light is extinguished appears to be the signal for a mass exodus. That's when cognitive dissonance takes charge. Don't even entertain the notion.

*CARDINAL SIN*

One terrible sin, however, should be singled out as a dreadful example, without being buried in some sub-category. It's *Advertising That Aims Itself At a Youth Market* and makes the following assumptions: first, that because we are talking to young people, we should show young people; and, second, because we are talking to young people who like lots of enthusiasm and wackiness, we should exhibit lots of enthusiasm and wackiness.

Oh heavens, you say to yourself, there he goes again: the man is obsessed. Of course advertising should be enthusiastic and wacky. So we have the same principles but two different interpretations.

*Q:* How do you explain the proliferation of ads where young people are portrayed being young and energetic, on the assumption that (a) young people will know the brand is for them, and (b) the youth and energy will transfer themselves to the ad and therefore the brand?

It doesn't work like that. Ads featuring athletic young people being energetic are so typical of muddled marketing thinking that no one even queries them. There are plenty of ways that resourceful creatives can make an ad energetic without resorting to ecstatic young people (in the form of healthy models with perfect teeth) being enthusiastic about the product.

The reason that no one even queries the format is that this battered cliché constitutes the mainstream of international advertising content.

When post-modernism grabbed modernism's crown, decay became the dominant creative style. Under the new ruler, clarity suffered, buried under layers of irony and ornament. The message became muffled. The golden age had been transmuted into brass.

TV advertising, now old enough to possess a past, became self-referential and, obeying McLuhan's observation, began to consume itself. As Paul McCann wrote:[23]

**23** The *Independent*, 20 April 1988.

*Advertising will eat itself. After years of taking the mickey out of other famous advertising campaigns or making a pastiche of movies, recent campaigns have started looking to themselves for their ideas.*

*The latest TV advert from Tango, which is always a benchmark for the hippest trends in the world of advertising, shows a lowly advertising executive being reprimanded by his female boss for his last Tango ad: 'The clown ad wasn't good enough. People didn't get it.' She makes the poor exec get into a cupboard with her, where some unspeakable punishment is exacted on him. He leaves the cupboard in tears, and the advert ends with the slogan: 'No more rubbish Tango ads. Ever.'*

*This follows hard on the heels of a Chicken Tonight advert which made fun of the cook-in-sauces' nightmare signature tune. Chicken Tonight, when first advertised in the UK, used a song from its American agency – 'I feel like Chicken Tonight' – that if played often enough could induce large-scale emigration.*

Self-reference was everywhere. Parodies became commonplace, applauded and rewarded. The extraneous kitsch and unnecessary ornamentation binned by the classic school was revived as the essence of post-modern ads. Faced with a new generation that prided itself on being ironic, ads started addressing irony itself. Image had become confused with imagery, advertising with art, and the iconography was talking to a mirror.

In a post-modern world, nothing is the same any more. I read the the following article once. Then I read it again. When Procter & Gamble start to practise what some of us have preached for years, what will their wannabes do? P&G's traditional approach was to:

> *... put a lot of media out there, put a good product out there, and tell them to buy it. Now [P&G] recognizes change... Executions now have a lot more emotional value added. Individualized marketing based on interactive relationships of mutual respect. And that requires quite dramatic changes in the way we go to market.*[24]

Am I being unduly pessimistic about current creative practices? Are these the ramblings of a cynical old copywriter who should have been put out to grass?[25] Well, not when my views are receiving corroboration from that admirable style commentator, Peter York, the man who helped invent Sloane Rangers. When reviewing a Famous Grouse commercial (isn't that appropriate?), he wrote:[26]

**24** Paul Polman, UK General Manager of Procter & Gamble, as quoted from *Campaign*, 20 March 1998.

**25** And would I have asked such questions if I didn't have a ready answer?

**26** The *Independent on Sunday*, 12 January 1997.

*The whole thing has the feeling of the best seventies ads. I sense that young creatives have been watching a lot of the best stuff from that period, in reaction to nineties New Age and Hypertech.*

And, as though *he* needed any corroboration, one of the more outspoken of advertising's Young Turks, creative director Trevor Beattie, present at the birth of both the 'Hello Boys' posters for Wonderbra and 'FCUK advertising' for French Connection, said in a *Guardian* interview:

*If you spend £6 million on a car campaign and no one can even remember the name of the car, then you should have given the money to cancer research, because there's a proper cause. There are loads of ads around that don't tell people about the product – or even what the product is. I don't think that's cool, I think it's crap. What's the point of being so obtuse?*

To which we can only add, in chorus: what *is* the point of being so obtuse? And so bloody precious?

It will hardly have gone unnoticed that Step 9 has been crammed with do's and don'ts, all worthy of close revision, as are the mega-propositions below.

# REVISE AND NEVER FORGET

### Proposition No. 38

*Fashion is not an idea.*

### Proposition No. 39

*If we're in the reminder business, keep it simple.*

### Proposition No. 40

*'Tell a story, man.'*
*Lester Young*

# STEP 10: SACRIFICE

It is a little-known fact that the very moment you approve a new advertising campaign, your hard-wired Prayer Dispatch System (PDS)[1] with autopilot-controlled circuitry simultaneously beseeches the gods to intercede favourably on your behalf.

Students of religious practices will vouch that all Premier League deities insist on a genuine sacrifice as a token of your belief and commitment. In this case, '*genuine*' means something precious (as in '*valuable*', not the other kind). In primitive societies, '*precious*' was an ox, a sheep or a human virgin.

Students of marketing practices will note that, in post-primitive societies, this sacrifice has altered into a different form: instead of livestock or an unwilling human, small green paper sheets are incinerated in bulk. Often, also unwillingly.

As with all burnt offerings, there's no guarantee that it will perform as planned. Whether or not your brand will succeed was determined some time before. *The sacrifice only marks the conclusion of the final rite.*

So the next question could well be worth a massive conflagration of anyone's money.

*Q:* How do you actually judge an ad in script, rough or storyboard form?

1   Typical PDS message encodings: '*Please God, I'll do anything You want if You…*', '*Please God, I'll stop doing anything You want if You…*', '*Please God, I promise to be good if You…*'.

*A:* We start with the Dogmatic route.

**Comment:** This elegant beast is named Mel.[2]

At least, that's what his friends call him, because his pedigree name, registered at the Kennel Club, is *Saredon Forever Young*. Mel is the most perfect specimen of a Welsh Terrier extant. His tail is the prescribed length, to a millimetre. Every dimension of his muzzle fits the breed book specification to a T. His paws are flawless and his glossy red coat drives doggie experts orgasmic down to their sensible shoes.

He was, in fact, Champion of Champions Crufts 1998, and was judged so by a distinguished panel of canine gurus. That's how you judge dogs. Unfortunately, that's not how you judge *ads*.[3]

2    Apparently named after an Australian film actor.

3    Proposition No. 41: Don't judge ads the way you judge dogs.

By '*judging*', I don't mean whether or not the ads should be included in the Design & Art Direction annual or the latest Cannes ad film festival reel. Not that kind of judging. I'm talking about judging whether they're *fit to run*. Whether they have your authority to preach your gospel. Whether they can persuade sceptical, apathetic consumers about the virtues of your brand. Whether they make a genuine contribution to the brand myth. Whether they take your business forward.

## BLACK HOLES

Normally, when ads are being judged, even professionals experience doubt. In which case, you need a lot of help, so make sure you don't leave home without:

◆ *common sense;*

◆ *a sharpened eye;*

◆ *a tuned ear;*

◆ *a portfolio of serious experience;*

◆ *a sense of humour;*

◆ *a short list of intelligent criteria;*

◆ *a sense of purpose; and*

◆ *your consumer looking over your shoulder.*

*Warning:* Unfortunately, as we can see all around us every day, there is no foolproof way to avoid bummers. Nor is there any foolproof method of writing them out of your life totally (speaking as one who has been responsible for the odd one).[4]

4  Encouraged? It's amazing how many calamities occur because '*it seemed like a good idea at the time*'.

Another recommendation: It's best to avoid taking decisions in any atmosphere that resembles group hysteria. Group hysteria, responsible for some nasty, warped and bizarre decisions, prompted Nietzsche to observe: '*In individuals, insanity is rare. In groups, nations and committees, it is the rule.*'

And here's another. Enter the fray in a positive manner. And remember: very few clients are brave enough to brief an agency – as does Ian McAllister, chairman of the Ford Motor Company – to '*have the courage to produce work that I personally might not like*'.

Finally some reassurance. It is perfectly normal to:

◆ *doubt;*
◆ *seek safeguards and protection against the unknown;*
◆ *study the portents; and*
◆ *exhaust the arguments,*

before you to commit to exposing your message to the greater congregation. It also doesn't half strengthen your hand to have some good questions tucked up your sleeve. And here they come. *(Dear Reader: realizing that most of the advice about to be dispensed seems to concern commercials, please don't fret. The principles apply universally to any medium.[5])*

## ELEVEN RULES

These eleven handy rules (easy to remember, expensive to forget) will make it less likely that you are throwing your money into a very large, very hot and very inexhaustible barbecue.

**5**  Here's a useful piece of pro advice: even if posters aren't on the schedule, ask for poster designs. Because, says **Proposition No. 42: If you can't say it on a poster, you can't say it in any medium.**

*QUESTION NO1: IS THE LIFE FORCE PRESENT?*

*Q:* Do you sniff a bit of danger in the execution?

*A:* Depending on who you are, this could be a good or a bad signal.

*Comment: Good* because danger equals excitement, and excitement means the presence of energy. *Bad* because the execution in question may be yours.

All right, sorry, a bad joke. But with good intention. If a little danger in the air imperils your career, then you are confronted with a choice. If your reaction is: 'This is great, but they'll never buy it,' then go with it and make your name. If you feel 'This must go no further,' then reject it, stay where you are and be safe for as long as you can.[6]

If you're on the side of goodness, we'll continue. If this presentation caused a tingle, are you able to isolate its source?

- ◆ *The script?*
- ◆ *The design?*
- ◆ *The posters?*
- ◆ *The wit?*
- ◆ *The* chutzpah?
- ◆ *The presentation?*
- ◆ *The music?*

6  If you responded with the second option, go back a few pages and see how P&G are coping with a new climate.

◆ *The images?*

◆ *The opportunities?*

◆ *Or is it the whole thing?*[7]

**7**   *Der Gestalt*, as the
       Germans put it.

'The whole thing' is the answer to crave, with all the components precisely intermeshed. Everything working together.

*Q:* Intermeshed and working together to what end?

*A:* The creation of energy.

**Comment:** Energy isn't necessarily flash, clash and brash. **You don't have to be loud, flamboyant or noisy to communicate energy**[8] (think how the low-key entrance of Beethoven's Fifth creates tension and menace).

**8**   Proposition No.
       43.

Advertising containing genuine energy communicates easily (think about your annual sales conference; now, think about how much effort you put into communicating energy in order to convince the salesforce.[9])

**9**   Sales conferences I
       have attended and
       comment I have
       overheard:

       Marketing Director
       (about sales force):
       'Cynical? You don't
       know the half of it.'
       Salesman (after
       marketing director's
       speech): 'Same old
       bollocks, year after
       year.'

But what if you don't smell danger? What happens when it goes the other way, the Route of The Damp Squib? Let's assume you've examined the proposed advertising campaign, up and down and inside out for a few hours. Yes, it says all the right things. Yes, it says them in a slightly unusual way. Yes, it's resourceful, even ingenious. But it leaves you cold.

A succession of images to music might look good at the presentation, but if it's disguising a lack of content, it's nothing but a blob. It'll never sell anything.

Great ads are self-evident.

But I don't hold with that precious notion that the creative department and only the creative department can be the sole trustees of the creative flame. One of the most successful launches with which I have ever been involved was a new product for Mary Quant cosmetics at the end of the sixties. The technical staff had produced a range of cosmetics that were almost smudge-proof, and the brand manager called it *'Make-up to Make Love In'*. It made developing the ads almost easy.

Travelling back even further, there was the famous occasion when the Milk Marketing Board client representative quite liked the presentation from Mather & Crowther but felt the ads lacked something. The agency's line was on the didactic side: 'Drink a pint of milk a day.' That night, seated on the loo while his bath was running in, the MMB man wrote on the steamy wall tiles: 'Drinka Pinta Milka Day'[10] and scribbled his way into advertising folklore.

**When the ads on the wall look as though they belong on the wall, you haven't got ads, you've got wallpaper.**[11] Wallpaper is a symptom that the Energy Quotient is ebbing – low or sadly lacking. Big tough brands will kick sand in its face.

10 *'Pinta'* found its way into the *Oxford English Dictionary*, an achievement I have never ceased to envy.

11 **Proposition No. 44**.

# SOLUTION? BUILD UP YOUR ADVERTISING'S ENERGY QUOTIENT.

Give your campaign more punch: no content means no comment.

Give your campaign a shape – at the very least a beginning, a middle and an end.

Give your campaign a structure, and style it in a way that interests your audience.

Exercise Brand muscle only: promote the brand, *not* the product, *nor* the category.

Build interest: capture attention, avoid monotony, surf tension and release like a good raconteur.

**Then...**

Apply dynamic tension: use drama, intrigue, fascination and mystery.[12]

The big secret? *Anticipation.* As old admen used to advise: '*Sell the sizzle, not the sausage.*' Anticipation is often far more stimulating than the real thing.

Take a seven-day free trial and see if life doesn't improve.

12   The great Stanhope Shelton used to say: *'Start your commercial with a surprise and build up to a climax'* – as good a definition of shape as any.

## QUESTION NO 2: DOES THE TALENT SHOW?

Harold Ross, the great editor who shaped the *New Yorker* magazine, set two criteria for his contributors:[13]

◆ *Is it funny?*
◆ *And if it isn't funny, is it interesting?*[14]

The Ross route is infallible.

If your agency is recommending some advertising based
around a joke, is the joke funny?

Or is it feeble? Feeble jokes were ancient when you heard them
in the playground. They come from that pathetic tradition
known as 'whimsy'. Feeble jokes evoke neither titter nor smile.
Instead of making you laugh, they make you groan. Or wince.

Some feeble jokes might have been funny before they were
censored, or filleted, or slightly emasculated to react to the sales
situation in the north-east. Few good jokes survive committees.

In the vicinity of ads, feeble jokes provoke a negative field: like
advertising Black Holes, they absorb all available energy, explaining why people in show business who need funny jokes employ
professional gag-writers. Real gag writing is a serious affair, a fine
art best left to the few people with genuine ability. Advertising
creatives, by and large, are not professional gag-writers.

13  His contributors
included some of
the greatest writers,
cartoonists,
humorists and critics
of the twentieth
century, including
Robert Benchley,
Dorothy Parker, S J
Perelman, James
Thurber, Peter
Arno, Chas
Addams, and so on
and so on.

14  **Proposition No.
45.**

If the joke isn't funny, scrap it. If you don't, the consumer will do the job for you.

Right, so the story's not funny. But is it interesting? And by interesting, I don't mean of interest to your brand owner, brand manager or competitors. I mean does your ad contain something that might be of genuine interest to your consumers?

News is novelty. News is powerfully motivating. People come to the media not just for entertainment but for information. Being in the know is important. If they're receptive to news, shouldn't you be giving them some? How much news does your campaign convey?

### Here is the news

'News', in advertising terms, means an effective reintroduction of the brand to the consumer. Examples? Have you recommended a fresh way of using your brand? Have you invested it with fresh significance? A design change? Improved performance? Lower price? A new method of consuming at a different time of day? Might it play a new role in the sex war?

The process of advertising is nothing more than a long conversation with your consumer. How long it continues is up to you. Ask yourself: how long can you converse with a bore?

Your consumer's interest should be tweaked. A little flirting to keep the relationship alive. A touch of spicy brand gossip (and how it might impinge on the consumer's life). A few pointers towards its future development.

Get the tone right, and you won't go wrong. As long as it's either interesting. Or funny. Or, better still, both.

*QUESTION NO. 3: DOES MONEY MATTER?*

If the campaign is utterly dependent on the images of famous personalities, can you afford them and are they available?

Too many films are written to include, but lack the presence of, a major actor or cult figure – who refuses to appear on-camera in a commercial.[15]

When most personalities are generally famous for being personalities, using stand-ins is a cop-out, an automatic charisma bypass. Gene Kelly's ecstatic gyrating in a downpour in *Singin' in the Rain*[16] is brilliant because Stanley Donen was a brilliant director, MGM spent an awful amount of money to get it right, and Gene Kelly is pretty damn inimitable. But botched imitations in an ad do the ad no good at all.

Therefore, if a campaign lives or dies on the presence of an unavailable megastar, axe the project instantly because it is doomed. Only the right star is the right star. As *stylemeister* Peter York has observed:[17]

15  They'll usually be more than happy to take your money for voice-overs.

16  An instance chosen because the Cannes jury on which I served was exposed to at least half-a-dozen botched imitations from all over the world, each greeted by lacklustre Bronx cheers.

17  Peter York, *Independent on Sunday*, 15 February 1998.

*[Actors/comedians] have another advantage. Research shows that they're seen to have a quite different, less compromised relationship with the advertiser than star spokesmen do. In the primeval days of American television, stars like Ronald Reagan and Doris Day would do a turn straight to camera on the advertiser's glories; they'd even do personal testimonials of the 'my wife swears by it' variety. You hardly ever see that now – especially on British TV. Stars are used more obliquely, parodically, iconically. Research also shows that a more sophisticated audience – and all viewers speak marketing-speak now – simply tends not to believe a straight pitch.*

*In any case, a straight pitch runs the risk of mismatching brand personalities. People can turn off the product because they can't identify with the star – Not Quite Our Class Darling or Not Quite Our Fashion Speed. But used obliquely as a statement, a reference or something of the kind, the agency can cover itself against any kind of research reading.*

*If you want a star as your spokesman or spokeswoman, you have to think through the boxes very carefully – Product Compatibility, Audience Identification, Sustainability, Insurance Against Death, Drama or Sun (Glen Hoddle vanished promptly from his family breakfast cereal gig when the tabloids ran the story about his marriage going south).*

Which matter brings us to the next point:

**Q:** Are you saddling yourself with an unachievable script?

**Comment:** It's your money, and you're fully entitled to demand value and insist on scrutinizing the estimate. But bear in mind the big *'however'* lurking behind that statement: penny-pinching in movie-making can jeopardize a film's effectiveness.

Study the script carefully if you don't want to be handicapped with an execution too ambitious for the budget, otherwise you'll be sorry later. No crowd scene can be assembled when the budget stretches only to two extras; it will look tacky and will bear scant resemblance to *Ghandi* or *Titanic*. And you don't want to end up screening *The Magnificent Four, Singin' in the Drizzle* or *Lawrence of the Sandpit.*

You know that blockbuster spot for Blackcurrant Tango? The one with the sales director stripping his clothes in the rain and changing into boxing gear, accompanied by crowds, Harrier jump jets and the White Cliffs of Dover? Would it have worked on a smaller budget? (Incidentally, with ironic xenophobia as its theme, would you have bought it?)

What sounds like a high flyer at the presentation often metamorphoses into a turkey if the money and the will aren't present. Find the money and the will. Leave all turkeys to Bernard Matthews.

QUESTION NO. 4: ARE THE SEEDS OF IMMORTALITY DETECTABLE?

**Q:** Does this idea have legs? Can it run for ever? Is it, at the very least, campaignable?

**Comment:** Remember this: very, very few campaigns spring famous and mature at first appearance. Viewed from today's perspective, the first British Heineken commercials were, executionally, very ploddy. But the idea was clear, the commitment was consistent, and the campaign took wing.

British Telecom has frequently had immortality in its hand: *Busby*, '*It's for Yoo-Hoo*', Maureen Lipman as Beattie,[18] but no serious consistent attempt at defining BT's personality. Consequently (and I'm fully aware that I'm being subjective), I've never encountered anyone who felt really good about BT. And I know I can't find it in my heart to love them.

**Recommendation:** Ask about subsequent treatments. You may never use them, but they demonstrate how the campaign can grow. They also force the agency to sift content from style and isolate what will make the campaign work. If the central thought is complex and arcane, don't waste your money. If the idea is simple and universal, it has a future.

**Another recommendation:** Some agencies sneakily present campaigns in *Year One* and *Year Two* form. *Year One* establishes the theme in a slightly clumpy manner. *Year Two* usually takes the theme, adds some spice, and makes it interesting. The agency in question would really like to start with *Year Two*, but the Year One executions have been inserted so that the idea is clearly

18  It took me years to realize that it was an intentional pun: *Beattie = BT*. Oh, forget it.

understood by people like your chairman and financial director. My advice: run *Year Two* now.

**Q:** Is the idea different:  ☐ original, or ☐ unusual? (Please tick whichever is applicable.)

**Comment:** If you've left both boxes unticked, then the odds are against your idea leaping off screen, page or billboard. If it isn't different, original or unusual, then it must be clichéd, unoriginal or bland. In which case, at best, it might well be confused with some other brand's communication and, at worst, it will be ignored.

Invisible looks bad on the balance sheet. Please don't waste your money.

QUESTION NO. 5: IS THE IDEA RIGHT FOR THE BRAND?

Or is it perched there uncomfortably like a bishop in a brothel?

**Comment:** There are few things on earth more embarrassing than a well-worn brand trying to be trendy. Judging relevance, congruity and tonality depends on the specific brand and how the agency is planning to revive its fortunes.

**Recommendation:** Be wise, diplomatic and bold. But here's a thought to ponder: many brands have notched great sales with emotional advertising that they hesitate to alter. Yet, occasionally, even the best-managed brands need a tweak of the rational–emotional joystick.

Sometimes, you have to reconvince new audiences that there is a very good rational reason to prefer your brand over the competition. If you're able to blend the rational and emotional seamlessly, then you're on to a winner.

QUESTION NO. 6: IS THIS A VAMPIRE-FREE ZONE?

**Q:** Is the idea inextricably linked with the brand? Or, to put it another way, are you being asked to buy an idea for some other brand?

**Recommendation:** Using your hand or a sheet of agency notepad,[19] excise your brand from the script or storyboard. Now here comes the acid test. Could the ad be used by someone else? If it could, then someone might well be about to use it – perhaps even your most feared competitor. Your advertising should be yours alone, and preferably unique. Yet it can never be so if its attraction rests on borrowed interest.[20] *Your ad must be your ad.*[21]

*Warning.* As much as agencies spout airily about 'big ideas', *the really great advertising ideas have always been those that can't survive without the brand.*[22] You can borrow interest by placing a large false moustache across your upper lip, but it's the moustache that will be noticed, not you. Similarly, when borrowing interest, an extraneous attention-getting device is appliquéd onto your advertising. And because the attention-getting device exists solely to attract all the attention, that's where all the attention may rest. So, unfortunately your brand stands every chance of being forgotten.

19  At last, a use for it.

20  Aka vampire video (a term coined by Rosser Reeves), which sucks the blood out of your message by being too interesting in its own right.

21  Proposition No. 46.

22  Proposition No. 47.

*QUESTION NO. 7: ARE YOU BEING OVER-EARNEST?*

Mythical conversation, held any time in the last half-century.

*Scene: an agency boardroom somewhere.*

*Agency:* Well then, what strap line really sums up your attitude towards your consumer?

*Client:* We care.

*Press 'pause' button and wait for comment.*

**Comment:** Life is hard (and that's why there's entertainment). Life is also boring, tedious, repetitious and dull (and that's why there's art). Unless you're in daytime TV running infomercials, lighten up. No brand was built on didactics. Furthermore, your personal enthusiasm for the brand, however deeply felt, doesn't transfer to advertising in any way motivating to consumers. What starts as a joke can lapse into farce.

*Press 'start' button and resume action.*

*Agency (incredulously): We care?*

*Client:* Absolutely. You asked us to provide a summation of our attitude towards the consumer and that's it. Now that you ask, what we really want is a line that says, er, um, you know, '*We care.*'

*Agency:* What, like British Airways' old 'We take good care of you'?

*Client (tetchily):* There's no need to be insolent…

*Agency (warming to task):* Or the classic, 'Securicor care'?

23     You mean you've never noticed?

*Client (aghast):* You mean Securicor says 'We care'?[23]

*Agency:* Right. Squads of burly ex-coppers wearing body armour and helmets with visors, carrying threatening truncheons. And their armoured vans carry the legend: 'Securicor care'. Anyone for cognitive dissonance?

The desire to say 'we care' is not uncommon. It generally signals frustration with the lack of progress in projecting an image. But as soon as a client tells me that he cares, I start counting the silver. Something tells me that the insistence to instill such an image into my consciousness might serve to mask the precise opposite, as when someone tells you that you are nice, or have style. It's a set of words you cannot use about yourself and expect to be believed. And yet some clients have insisted.

Maybe it's because some clients get frustrated with their campaign failing to communicate its main theme clearly. Sometime it's a symptom of a client wanting to hide the less attractive facets of his business (try: Securicor). Sometimes it's a symptom of client frustration at not getting the message across.

In April 1998, I snapped this emphatic version of 'we care' on the side of a container lorry in England's furthermost south-eastern corner. It's the *'seriously'* that really gets me. It's almost as though the writer knows that 'taking care' will be disbelieved, so that he or she has added 'seriously' to underline the thought that it is a genuine, heartfelt sentiment.

*Spotted near Mousehole, Cornwall. I like the 'seriously'*

I'd guess that the 'caring' rot set in during the seventies, when international agencies persuaded clients with the mega-macho marketing concept of 'global advertising'. It seemed that part of the global advertiser's survival kit was a vocabulary of pidgin lines, resulting in mangled English strap lines such as *'Martini is'* and *'Coke is it'*. Suddenly, intelligent brand summations dipped from copy fashion, and consumers were bombarded with a stream of 'Be there', 'Reach out', 'Go for it' and 'The Big One'.[24]

24 Once at a travel conference, I challenged the audience to identify airlines by their strap lines. Beneficiaries of millions of pounds of advertising were unable to guess one correctly. My personal favourite of all time: Pan-Am's cracker during the 1970s: 'We fly the world the way the world wants to fly'. In an aircraft, perhaps?

In my opinion, *'we care'* is actually the ultimate *de rigeur* brand affirmation for all deeply concerned corporations from suppliers of hit men to armament and land-mine conglomerates. They really *care*. **Never underestimate credibility.**[25]

*QUESTION NO. 8: AM I BEING POMPOUS?*

**Q:** Why do generations of TV viewers guffaw at the portrayal of Captain Mainwaring in the immortal BBC sitcom *Dad's Army*?[26]

**A:** Because he's an instantly recognisable portrait of a monumentally pompous person.

**Comment:** Pomposity is the act of taking oneself seriously.

When pomposity becomes intertwined with the act of boasting in public, it becomes fraught with embarrassment. The result is that many self-obsessed advertisers, petrified at the thought of causing offence, say very little of interest (except to themselves).

Pomposity explains the tonality of early advertising, namely the self-conscious voice of the cautious merchant not wanting to upset the middle-class sensibilities of their customers. Anxious not to lose face, the result usually emerged as self-importance, ill at ease.

For all the reasons previously stated, pompous clients loathe humour in advertising. Understandably. In Britain, humour deals in the absurd, in ridicule, and in poking fun at human foibles and authority. In short, it's anarchic.

**25** Proposition No. 48.

**26** The most unlikely of funny World War II situations: when the aged, the infirm and the unfit were enlisted to defend Britain from imminent Nazi invasion.

Humour in advertising is either a) intentional or b) unintentional.[27] Inevitably, b) gives rise to a lot more hilarity than a).[28] But more inevitably comes the question that clients ask agencies: 'Why *must* it be funny?'

*Comment:* Late one night, I watched a TV Euro chat show hosted by Clive James. After James had made a witty and telling point about the topic under discussion (audience laughter), a learned German guest asked why he joked about something so serious. Single-handedly illuminating the problem that Brits have with the German sense of humour, Clive James returned the question: 'Are you saying that serious issues must be solemnly treated?'

'Yes,' responded the German, 'in Germany we do not joke about serious subjects.'[29] James looked at him with the expression of a man who has a honed riposte: 'Ah, but in Britain joking is a serious matter.'

Dealing lightly and wittily with serious issues has long been a speciality of consummate copywriter David Abbott. He once wrote an ad for a trade union under the headline: '*The Board and I have decided we don't like the colour of your eyes.*' And for an ad dealing with firework abuse, under a picture of a bandaged youth, he ran this line: '*Make sure the wrong guy doesn't get burnt tonight.*'

*Pomposity in advertising breeds blandness.*[30] (If we return to our original religious theme, we observe that when religions become bland, adherents fall away.) Bland is boring, commonplace and trite. Devoid of imagination, it is decidedly unromantic and unattractive. Bland is the diametrical opposite of what

27  The largest company of undertakers in South Africa, where I grew up, was called Human & Pitt.

28  It creates cults like the 'Ambassador's Reception' for Ferrero Rocher where wrapped chocolates are handed to a group of unlikely models.

29  This is further corroborated by my German chum, Claus Koch, who told me that his agency invited all the major German marketing directors to a preview of that year's Cannes prizewinning reel. They all fell about applauding and laughing at all the winners, while commenting '*Of course, you can't do that in Germany.*'

30  **Proposition No. 49.**

most people want. Folks out there enjoy the theatrical. They like a bit of drama and make-believe. Brand personality is displayed at its best when it allows people to play and pretend. And nobody wants to pretend to be bland.

While I have no evidence to support my claim, I would suggest that even bland people want to be loved. The problem is that they don't know how to attract love. Beauty, charm and sexiness attract it.[31] Those deficient in all those categories should avoid begging for love and go for admiration instead.

31  A combination of all three is lethal. And if you feel that describes you, then why are you reading this book?

But, for heaven's sake, never appear to be courting it. At the first sniff of desperation, your target market switches off.

The trick? Start off cool. Be exclusive. People should want you, not you them. Anyone trying to recruit should remember the great sage of the 20th century: Marx. *Groucho,* that is: 'I don't want to join any club that would have me as a member.'

32  Don't ask. Lots.

My experience in the drinks business[32] taught me that the best way to launch a product is not to allow the advertisements to define its role, usage and audience too tightly. Telling the whole story, revealing the entire plot, as you see it on first airing, is unwise. You may be ascribing a character to a brand that doesn't sit happily on its shoulders. And that's something many brand-owners have later regretted.

***Recommendation:*** In fact, the brand should stand aloof. Exclusive. Cool. And because it is so vital to alert the early adopters, the art in designing the campaign resides in finding the coolest possible way of easing yourself into their view. Because, unless you interest *them*, no one will follow.

QUESTION NO. 9: ARE YOU ASKING AN AD TO DO TOO MUCH?

**Q:** If you were the Deity, what sort of appeal would invite your wholehearted intervention? A single passionate plea? Or a bullet-pointed agenda that disguises personal requirement (*'Please let me have a good meeting tomorrow'*) with a public-spirited issue (*'Please save the whales and stop all diseases in Africa'*)?

**Comment:** the Formula One racing car is a machine specifically designed to perform in a highly competitive environment. It is extremely efficient, highly machined, carefully constructed and very quick. However, it is hardly capacious. No one would dream of collecting the weekly supermarket shopping in a Formula One machine.

In fact, each car is destined to run one race only before it is taken apart and reconstructed. Formula One cars are not required to perform any other function except that which they are designed to do (other than carry a range of brand names). If you treat an ad like a Formula One car, you won't go far wrong. It is not meant to be a multi-purpose vehicle. It should be custom-tailored, custom-built. Designed to win.

If your main message needs lots of factual support, you would do well to make each piece of support the subject of a single ad. Like one of those Swiss army knives, which promises to perform a huge range of functions in an emergency, overloading a communication makes it inefficient.

A Swiss army knife can never be a primary tool. It cannot be as efficient as a purpose-designed screwdriver or proper scissors or a professional fish-scaler. It is brilliant only at being a stand-by, multi-purpose instrument – in effect, a useful toy. The desire to make a single instrument perform a multitude of functions fills me with dread. Likewise with ads.

In 1963, when I was very new to the business and working at a Dickensian advertising agency in a garret perched above High Holborn, London, I was instructed to travel to Norwich and attend the recording of a commercial being put on primitive videotape for regional transmission. The brand on test was a German kitchen-sponge-cum-abrasive-pad named Atomcoll (I'll spare you the tasteful mushroom-cloud logo).

The British client was eager to include some film footage that had come from the manufacturer (free of charge). The script (mostly written by the client to make optimum use of the free footage) promised consumers the sun, moon *and stars*. Atomcoll would not only scour the hairs off female legs (*cut to woman's leg with sponge delicately rubbed up and down*) but also (*cut to manufacturer's footage*) scrub squashed flies from windscreens ('*Brunhilde, this gotterdammerung sponge won't scrape the flies from my windscreen because it is clogged with your extraneous leg hairs.*').

I think the brand bombed right there in East Anglia. I never saw it on sale anywhere. And I managed to escape the agency before anyone ever asked for a second commercial.

*Question No. 10: Am I overloading the Communication?*

**Q:** Who's responsible for overloading communications?

**A:** People who ought to know better.

**Comment:** Overloaded advertising stems from top-heavy, over-eager briefing.

An advertising brief can be much more than a request for a new ad or campaign. Sometimes, it begs the agency to communicate your fervour about your brand. To write a successful brief is a special skill. Once you've dealt with all your anxieties, a brief should pose a problem that only a creative mind can solve. It should be inspiring and provide a launching pad for creative invention.

To an agency about to commit itself to creation, the brief is the Holy Writ, endlessly analysed ('What do they *really* mean?'), often reinterpreted ('Is *that* what they really want?'), and often totally misunderstood. Because, unfortunately, the world is full of advertising constructed on the wrong brief.

The agency, which has the job of harmonizing client intentions with consumer perceptions, also has to make allowances for client prejudices and the current state of corporate dogma. All in a moral environment which is constantly reshaping its envelope[33] (the world is running campaigns that could never have been run 20 years ago).

33  Twenty years ago you were not allowed to mention menstruation, pregnancy or condoms on British TV. Nor were you permitted to depict homosexuality. TV charity ads weren't allowed either.

Under these dynamic circumstances, there are countless opportunities for elephant traps. If you're lucky, success is dependent on agency skill and professionalism to save the day. But keep it simple.

QUESTION NO. 11: HAVE I SAID THE WRONG THING?

Language needs watching all the time. Here are some choice phrases to avoid:

a) *Try not to say, when confronted by long copy, 'Nobody reads all that guff.'* If the ad's interesting, people will read it. But if the ad's boring, they won't.

If you were confronted with the scribbled ad on the next page you'd read it, very carefully, word for word, because it exposes your deepest, darkest secrets.

When you're in the market for a new car, there are times when you want information rather than glitzy image. When you're making a considered purchase, you want confirmation and you'll eagerly consume as many words as there are, sometimes frequently sending off for more.

In certain markets, such as cosmetics (but not skin care), liquor, perfume, fashion and tobacco, long copy is probably a waste of time. In other markets, such as automotive, enthusiast wares, charities and health products, it might be a good idea.

But, never forget, people love a story. And they'll go to great lengths to hear one.

This is a list
of everyone
you've ever fancied.
Conquests are
underlined.

Who doesn't read long copy?

34    Did you know that the French themselves don't use the term *cul-de-sac*? They say *voie sans issue*.

b) '*Look at what Coke do.*' Watch out for irrelevant comparisons. To compare one brand with another, even to draw lessons from other successes and failures, can lead you into a *cul-de-sac*.[34] In my booze experience, young managers responsible for brands have bracketed them with Coca-Cola, Marlboro or Levi's. But very few factors are comparable.

Some brands of alcohol are bought once a year.

Unit price is different. And where cigarette and soft drinks ads and displays are almost permanent, some booze media appearances can have twelve months between bursts.

It's also worth remarking that advertising investment into Levi's, Marlboro and Coke have been substantial for nearly half a century.

However, what we can learn from these brands is that their success and power were built through unflagging, consistent application of their iconography. Without it, they would be nothing.

c) *Never utter: 'Let's put it out to research.'* Sad, really. I've seen strong admen reduced to tears. Like this:

Big pitch. Five agencies involved, all star studded. First round.

Clients go into purdah to confer. Long deathly hush.

Suddenly, puffs of papal white smoke appear, reading: 'Loved it all, but we're narrowing the field to two.'

Three losers retreat, mumbling imprecations.

Last two battle it out on slight rebrief. Two presentations made.

Clients depart saying, 'We'll let you know after the weekend.'

A week later, agency nails are gnawed to the shoulder.

Attempting to make contact with prospects is continually thwarted, forcing rival agency chairmen to call one another to scratch for gossip.

Finally, puffs of white smoke issue from the Vatican chimney: *'We're putting it out to research. May the best campaign win.'*

Perhaps this is where we part company. Perhaps you can define logic invisible to me. Perhaps you think that delegating the decision to a discussion group in Watford is a brilliant way to run a business. Do you also use the same discussion group to hire your staff? Or make your company vehicle purchase decisions.

In the end, like everything else, it's your opinion and your passion that should sway the day. And if you're wrong? Well, you can be pretty positive that they won't fire the discussion group in Watford.

*Q:* In this connection, have you ever wondered why creatives loathe research?

*A:* Because, in cynical hands, it can destroy radical campaigns.

Because it can reject an original idea that emerges twelve months later gathering notice and awards for someone else.

Because the cynics see it as a hit-and-miss technique for proving their ideas wrong.

Because they see it as an inefficient means of trying to gauge the future.

Because people much cleverer than myself have spotted its drawbacks: hearken to the opinions of Bernbach and Delano.[35]

First, Bill Bernbach:

*There is no such thing as a good or bad ad in isolation. What is good at one moment is bad at another.* **Research can trap you into the past.**[36]

And in the early eighties, Les Delano, the man who produced the very first campaign for Smirnoff vodka[37] (and who is still a major player in Lowes Worldwide) noted:[38]

*The US car industry has been tremendously maligned for its arrogance of purpose over the past twenty years.*

**35** See *Bill Bernbach Said.*

**36** **Proposition No. 50.**

**37** You want style? Smirnoff wanted to show that the brand made a perfect dry martini, so it sent Bert Stern, top Madison Avenue photographer, to Egypt to shoot the Grand Pyramid upside down through a martini glass.

**38** Address to Palm Beach, Florida, USA conference June 1981.

*They sat around saying that people should have big cars and that's all we're going to make, and while they were doing it, the Japanese were killing them.*

*I wonder if we're not really in the same position in our industry with our hardened procedural convictions, our contempt for theory as being unrealistic, our lack of hard work in trying to develop and improve our communication models.*

*Instead of clean, clear, crisp selling propositions, maybe we should be investigating ways to categorize and use things that appear to be chaotic and even heretical under our present rules.*

*After all, you know, there is ample evidence that such things as enigma, lack of closure, paradox, surprise, novelty and ambiguity can heighten tremendously the involvement aspects of a particular piece of communication.*

*Yet our standard techniques are devoted to their extinction.*

There you have it. But before you judge a single ad, make sure you revise your propositions thoroughly. And I hope it's all much clearer now.

# PROPOSALS TO REMEMBER

## 11 Questions

*1. Is the life force present?*

*2. Does the talent show?*

*3. Does money matter?*

*4. Are the seeds of immortality detectable?*

*5. Is the idea right for the brand?*

*6. Are we free of vampires?*

*7. Are you being over-earnest?*

*8. Are you being pompous?*

*9. Are you asking an ad to do to much?*

*10. Are you overloading the communication?*

*11. Do you make mistakes in criticism?*

### [And 10 more propositions]

### Proposition No. 41

*Don't judge ads the way you judge dogs.*

**Proposition No. 42**

*If you can't say it on a poster, you can't say it in any medium.*

**Proposition No. 43**

*You don't have to be loud, flamboyant or noisy
to communicate energy.*

**Proposition No. 44**

*When the ads on the wall look as though they belong on the wall,
you haven't got ads, you've got wallpaper.*

**Proposition No. 45**

*Is it funny? And if it isn't funny, is it interesting?*

**Proposition No. 46**

*Your ad must be your ad.*

**Proposition No. 47**

*The really great advertising ideas have always been those that can't
survive without the brand.*

**Proposition No. 48**

*Never underestimate credibility.*

## Proposition No. 49

*Pomposity in advertising breeds blandness.*

## Proposition No. 50

*'Research can trap you into the past'*
*Bernbach*

# STEP 11: ON THE OTHER SIDE

In an effort to spirit you, not only behind the scenes, but to penetrate right under the adfolk epidermis, I thought I'd link together three pieces I wrote some years ago for a weekly column in *Marketing* magazine. Contributed over a period of months, they form a loose trilogy inspired by agency paranoia. Please forgive me if I recycle my old obsessions at your expense.

## 1. POST PRESENTATION

'Phew. Thank heaven's that's over. Have they all gone?'

'They're being seen out of the front door at this moment.'

'Do you think they'll appoint us?'

'Who can tell?'

'Well, for what it's worth, I think the guy on the end liked the presentation.'

'Which one? Oh, the chain-smoking one with the suit like a crumpled J-cloth? He's Mr History. Spectacularly unimportant. He's the oily rag, a bag-carrier. Now the one who had his back to the door, that's Mr Big, he's Captain Decision.'

'Not if you believe the rumours. He's supposed to be on the transfer list. Hey... he scribbled something on his scratch-pad.'

'Quick: rub a pencil over it. What's it say?'

'It says "Check AGB", then it says "C2 mums" and then there's a little phallic squiggle and underneath it says "Book tickets".'

'Shit. Who's that at the door? They're not coming back, are they?'

'No. It's only the new business prospect escort unit returning from their see-the-buggers-off-the-premises duties. Hey guys, did their lips move? Did they mouth words like "Brilliant, you've won the business"?'

'Did they, hell. I've extracted more information from cockroach corpses.'

'Oh, *come on*. What about body language? Or subtly whispered asides?'

'Zilch. Sphinx-like. Unless you count his grateful thanks as I helped him on with his mac.'

'Do you think they liked it?'

'Well, since you beg my opinion, I think they hated the creative work, detested the media ideas, despised the promotional scheme, and thought our planning was a puddle of puppy poop.'

'That good? I'm not so sure the plump one in the grey and mauve striped tie wasn't enthusiastic.'

'Only when we fed him back the bits of the brief he gave us.'

'Shucks.'

'Anyway, we can always strip off the logos on the layouts and present them to someone else.'

'I thought that was how this campaign started.'

'Surely there was *some* word, *some* sign that they liked it. When did they say they'd get back to us?'

'Let's see. Their valedictory speech returns to haunt me in fragments of total recall: "We'd like to thank the agency for their obvious hard work in investigating the market (and we're the first to admit that it's a pretty unusual one, ha ha), and congratulate them on an unusual solution. As we explained in our letter, we are conducting a review involving a number of agencies including the incumbent, with whom we are not unhappy. We plan to discuss the various presentations over the weekend, and we should be getting back to you by the middle of next week, latest."'

'And the rest. They always set deadlines. And they always miss them.'

'And when they do, it goes something like this: "You made our choice very difficult. We saw so many solutions to our complex problem that the decision was not an easy one. Unfortunately, your agency was not..."'

'Quite honestly, I don't think their account would mesh happily with this agency.'

'You're right. Screw 'em. A drink?'

'Yeah, a large one. They don't deserve us.'

'Mmmm. But I wonder whether they'll appoint us?'

## 2. POST POST PRESENTATION

'Why don't they ring? It's been four – no three – days since they were in for the presentation. Didn't they say they'd make their minds up the next day? God. No news is bad news. Or is it *good* news? I can never quite remember.'

'Anyway, I don't think we won it. I mean, we would have heard, wouldn't we? That guy – the one down the end of the table with the woolly khaki tie – he never liked us. He asked the worst questions. Like that one about putting all their press money in TV. That was a stinker, maliciously inserted to distract me. Quite arrested my flow, log-jammed my drift. No sense of unfolding drama, silly sod.'

'The lady liked us though. Initially I'd a feeling she'd marked us down because we had too few women in the presentation team. But I could tell she warmed to me. Smiled a lot when I projected in her direction. Not unsexy, I thought. Couldn't take my eyes off her... God! Why haven't they rung yet? It's not as if we really need their lousy business. After all, it's only an account. Ad agencies are like revolving doors: one account leaves and another one follows, I mean, enters. Have you seen this year's free-fall figures? The income from their billing would make good the loss of those bastards from...'

'We won't get it. They hated the creative work. Detested it. They sneered at the ads. You would've thought they'd never seen a real commercial before. On the other hand, they'd asked us to be radical. Their brief advised ignoring all restraints. Still, I think it might have been wiser to check the script with the ITC before the presentation. The naked couple and the golden retriever might be a little rich even for today's audience.'

'Is our switchboard out of action or something? Run along and check. Find out whether Miss Twin Peaks is sitting at her desk paying attention. Or anything else, for that matter. She's so occupied melting the helmets of motorcycle couriers by flashing the north face of her boobs that she couldn't give a damn whether even Unilever was melting her switchboard begging us to accept their business. Unlike a certain other company I could name.'

'We spent a month assembling this presentation and now, a week – OK maybe three days – later, not a dicky-bird. Not a peep. Not a whimper. Not even one of those mysterious calls to the media department dishing them undercover dirt. Nothing. A soundless vacuum. In outer space, no one can hear me scream.'

'Perhaps we should have bribed them. Maybe we should have taped a few large denomination notes to the inside covers of their documents. Perhaps I should have nobbled the top man when he dashed out for a pee. Perhaps, perhaps, per-haps.'

'Quite frankly, I think they loathed the work. And my suit. And our media director. It didn't help that our creative (ho, ho) director completely cocked up the order of the story-boards. Or that our dizzy planner addressed the company by the wrong name, twice. At this instant they're obviously appointing someone else, because they have no wit, taste, imagination, discernment or balls.'

'I'm not so sure we'd be happy handling their business. They'd be terrible clients. Endless trips to their remote offices to niggle over a single word on a charity ad mechanical.'

'Stuff their lousy business. Probably seriously unprofitable. In fact, I shouldn't be surprised if they went belly up. I've heard some interesting City whispers concerning the bizarre hotel bedroom habits of their chairman. Apparently... *shit, is that the phone?*'

## 3. POST APPOINTMENT

'Well, people, guess what? They've just rung to inform me that we've won the business. Isn't that great! Thanks. I think it's time to release the odd cork.'

'Cheers. Oh, he did say there were one or two matters still open to discussion. They were uncertain about our creative solution. In fact, I think their head man made that clear at the presentation when he dropped his coffee cup into his lap at the key point, although his enthusiasm rallied when Samantha sponged him dry.'

'To be honest, the pathetic little solution we cooked up failed to ignite my imagination. I simply went along because it was all we had ten minutes before the prospect came in.'

'They weren't big on our media plan either. Blowing the entire budget on bus sides was a little radical in their eyes, and I'm inclined to agree with them. It was only an amusing idea, and we all know that amusing ideas have their roles in landing new business, but it was never practical. National TV is what they'd like to have (they say their dealers insist on it) but they've suffered a budget cut between their briefing and now, and they need to rejig available funds. Personally, I can't see it stretching to more than a low-level regional radio campaign, but that's showbusiness.'

'What? Yes, my glass is rather empty... thanks. Ah, just between us, they had another little niggle. Apparently, they weren't gobsmacked with Loretta. Now I know she's the person best suited for the job, but it seems they won't take kindly to a female account supervisor. I think we'll have to play them in slowly, but in the meantime Giles will run it – with Loretta observing.'

'Another drop? Why not? A little early, but what the hell. We don't win a piece of business every day. Or every month, for that matter! The boss man wasn't too keen on our planning. He felt our analysis was a tad superficial. Quite honestly, I agreed at the time, but I wasn't going to sabotage agency solidarity. It seems they have research they didn't reveal before the presentation...'

'How'd we win it? Simply that the other agencies involved were unreasonable, or so I'm told. Imagine their stupidity. They held fast to their presentations. Too rigid in their thinking. They refused to change personnel. They stood by their creative work. Can you believe it? No give. Integrity? Ha!'

'Now, of course, the income won't be everything we expected. They're cutting the budget and requesting a commission deal. Didn't I tell you? We've offered a substantial reduction. After all, how often do we gain accounts from clients of their magnitude? Wake up team, we're in business, y'know. So, we might have to fire a creative team or two, but that's life. Is there anything left in that last bottle?'

# INDEX